December
Making Books with Pockets

MW01056110

The series of monthly activity books you've been waiting for!

Enliven every month of the year with fun, exciting learning projects that students can proudly present in a unique book format.

Each month has lessons for art, writing, reading, math, science, social studies, and poetry.

Congratulations on your purchase of some of the finest teaching materials in the world.

For information about other Evan-Moor products, call 1-800-777-4362 or FAX 1-800-777-4332

Visit our website http://www.evan-moor.com. Check the Product Updates link for supplements, additions, and corrections for this book.

Authors: Jill Norris
                    Marilyn Evans
                    Jo Ellen Moore
Editor: Marilyn Evans
Copy Editor: Cathy Harber
Pocket Book Concept: Michelle Barnett,
                    Caitlin Rabanera
                    Ann Switzer
Illustrator: Jo Larsen
Designer: Cheryl Puckett
Desktop: Shannon Frederickson

Evan-Moor
EDUCATIONAL PUBLISHERS

EMC 595

December's Special Days

Here are ideas for celebrating some of the other special days in December.

December 5 _____ **Walt Disney's Birthday**
The creator of Mickey Mouse, Disneyland, and Disney World was born on this day in 1901. Divide into small groups to brainstorm and list as many Disney characters as you can.

December 6 _____ **St. Nicholas Day**
St. Nicholas was a real person who lived about 1600 years ago in Turkey. He became a special saint to children because of his many acts of kindness. In some European countries, St. Nicholas brings small gifts to children on this day. Surprise your students today with small packages of nuts and dried fruit left in their desks for them to find.

December 9 _____ **Birthday of Jean de Brunhoff**
Born in Paris in 1899, de Brunhoff is known as the author and illustrator of the stories about Babar, the elephant, and his wife, the good Queen Celeste. Enjoy one of the Babar tales.

December 13 _____ **St. Lucia Day**
Early on this morning, Swedish children deliver coffee and special buns to the adults in the house. The oldest girl, wearing a white robe and a crown of greenery with lighted candles, carries the tray. The other children follow, singing "Santa Lucia."

December 15 _____ **Beethoven's Birthday**
Born in Germany in 1770, Beethoven wrote some of the most exciting and well-known music in the world, much of it after he became totally deaf. Play part of one of his nine symphonies or his "Moonlight" sonata.

December 23 _____ **Night of the Radishes**
In the area around Oaxaca, Mexico, radishes sometimes grow as large as a child's arm. People carve figures and scenes out of radishes and display them in the city square. Prizes are given for the best radish sculpture. Bring in lots of radishes and challenge small groups to create radish sculptures.

December

Sunday	Monday	Tuesday	Wednesday	Thursday	Friday	Saturday

How to Make Pocket Books

Each pocket book has a cover and three or more pockets. Choose construction paper colors that are appropriate to the theme of the book. Using several colors in a book creates an effective presentation.

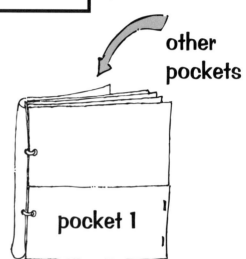

other pockets

pocket 1

Materials

- 12" x 18" (30.5 x 45.5 cm) piece of construction paper for each pocket
- cover as described for each book
- hole punch
- stapler
- string, ribbon, twine, raffia, etc., for ties

Steps to Follow

1. Fold the construction paper to create a pocket. After folding, the paper should measure 12" (30.5 cm) square.

2. Staple the right side of each pocket closed.

3. Punch two or three holes in the left side of each pocket and the cover.

4. Fasten the book together using your choice of material as ties.

5. Glue the poem or information strips onto each pocket as shown on the overview pages of each book.

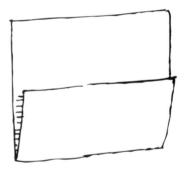

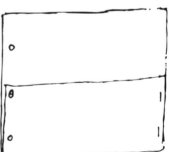

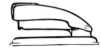

December Celebrations

The month of December is filled with wonderful celebrations. This pocket book highlights four of those celebrations—Las Posadas, Hanukkah, Christmas, and Kwanzaa. If your community celebrates a December holiday not included in this book, add an additional pocket.

This poem can also be used for pocket chart activities throughout the month:
- Chant the poem
- Listen for rhyming words
- Learn new vocabulary
- Identify sight words
- Put words or lines in the correct order

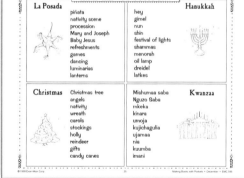

Use the picture dictionary to introduce new vocabulary and as a spelling reference. Students can add new pictures, labels, and descriptive adjectives to the pages as their vocabulary increases.

Use this form for story writing or as a place to record additional vocabulary words.

BIBLIOGRAPHY

Bookstores and libraries are filled with wonderful books about December celebrations. See the pocket overviews for a few recommended titles for specific holidays.

POCKET 1

**Celebrating
Las Posadas—A Miniposter**   **page 11**
Share this miniposter with facts about
Las Posadas.

In the Stable   **pages 12–14**
The charming donkey on the cover of this book
holds a lantern lighting the way to the safety of
his stable.

Paper Bag Luminaria   **page 15**
Students will love doing this writing project that
results in a luminaria to use as a decoration.

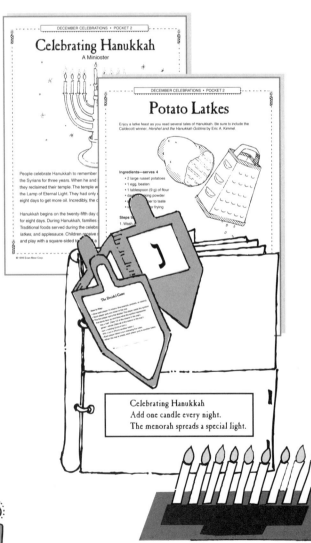

POCKET 2

**Celebrating Hanukkah—
A Miniposter**   **page 16**
Share this miniposter with facts about
Hanukkah.

Making a Menorah   **page 17**
Paper clip the base of the menorah to make it
stand by itself.

Dreidel   **pages 18–20**
Practice writing directions and play this
traditional Hanukkah game.

Potato Latkes   **page 21**
Enjoy these tasty latkes as you read Hanukkah
stories.

POCKET 3

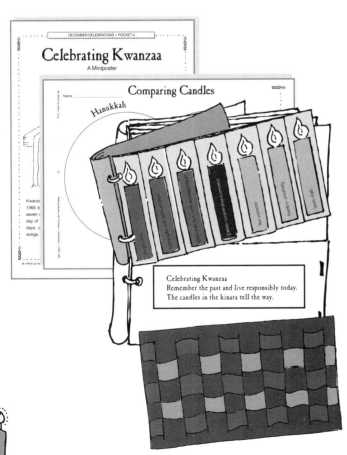

POCKET 4

BOOKS ABOUT LAS POSADAS

Carlos, Light the Farolito by Jean Ciavonne; Clarion Books, 1995.
Josefina's Surprise: A Christmas Story (American Girls Collection) by Valerie Tripp; Pleasant
    Company Publications, 1997.
The Legend of the Poinsettia by Tomie De Paola; Paper Star, 1997.
Nine Days to Christmas by Marie Hall Ets and Aurora Labastida; Viking Press, 1959.
Pancho's Piñata by Stefan Czernecki and Timothy Rhodes; Hyperion Books for Children, 1992.

BOOKS ABOUT HANUKKAH

All the Lights in the Night by Arthur Levine; Tambourine Books, 1991.
Elijah's Angel by Michael J. Rosen; Harcourt Brace Jovanovich, 1992.
A Hanukkah Treasury by Eric A. Kimmel; Henry Holt & Company, 1998.
Hershel and the Hanukkah Goblins by Eric A. Kimmel; Holiday House, 1985.
The Magic Dreidels: A Hanukkah Story by Eric A. Kimmel; Holiday House, 1997.
One Yellow Daffodil by David A. Adler; Gulliver Books, 1995.

BOOKS ABOUT CHRISTMAS

Bright Christmas: An Angel Remembers by Andrew Clements; Clarion Books, 1996.
The Christmas Ark by Robert D. San Souci; Doubleday, 1991.
The Christmas Miracle of Jonathan Toomey by Susan Wojciechowski; Candlewick Press, 1995.
The Christmas Tree Ship by Jeanette Winter; Paper Star, 1998.
The Grinch Who Stole Christmas by Dr. Seuss; Random House, 1957.
Santa's Book of Names by David McPhail; Little, Brown & Co., 1993.
Thank You, Santa by Margaret Wild; Scholastic, 1991.

BOOKS ABOUT KWANZAA

Celebrating Kwanzaa by Diane Hoyt-Goldsmith; Holiday House, 1993.
It's Kwanzaa Time by Linda and Clay Goss; Putnam, 1995.
Kwanzaa Fun by Linda Robertson; Kingfisher Books, 1996.
Seven Candles for Kwanzaa by Andrea Davis Pinkney; Dial Books for Young Readers, 1993.
The Story of Kwanzaa by Donna L. Washington; HarperCollins Juvenile Books, 1996.

Materials

- construction paper
  cover—dark blue, 12" (30.5 cm) square
  candle and title bars—pattern on page 10,
      reproduced on light blue for each student
  flame—yellow, 3" x 2" (7.5 x 5 cm)
- 6" x 2" (15 x 5 cm) gold foil wrapping paper
- 2" (5 cm) piece of pipe cleaner for wick

- gold metallic pen (optional)
- glue
- tape
- scissors
- black marking pen
- gold cording or ribbon

Steps to Follow

1. Cut out the two candle pieces. Position them on the cover.

2. Stick the pipe cleaner "wick" under the candle pieces. Tape it in position so that the tape does not show.

3. Glue the candle down.

4. Cut a flame from the yellow paper. Glue it over the pipe cleaner wick.

5. Round the ends of the gold paper to make a candleholder. Glue it over the base of the candle.

6. Outline the candle and the flame with the gold metallic pen.

7. Cut out the title bars and glue them to the cover.

8. Tie the pages together with gold cording or ribbon.

Candle Pattern

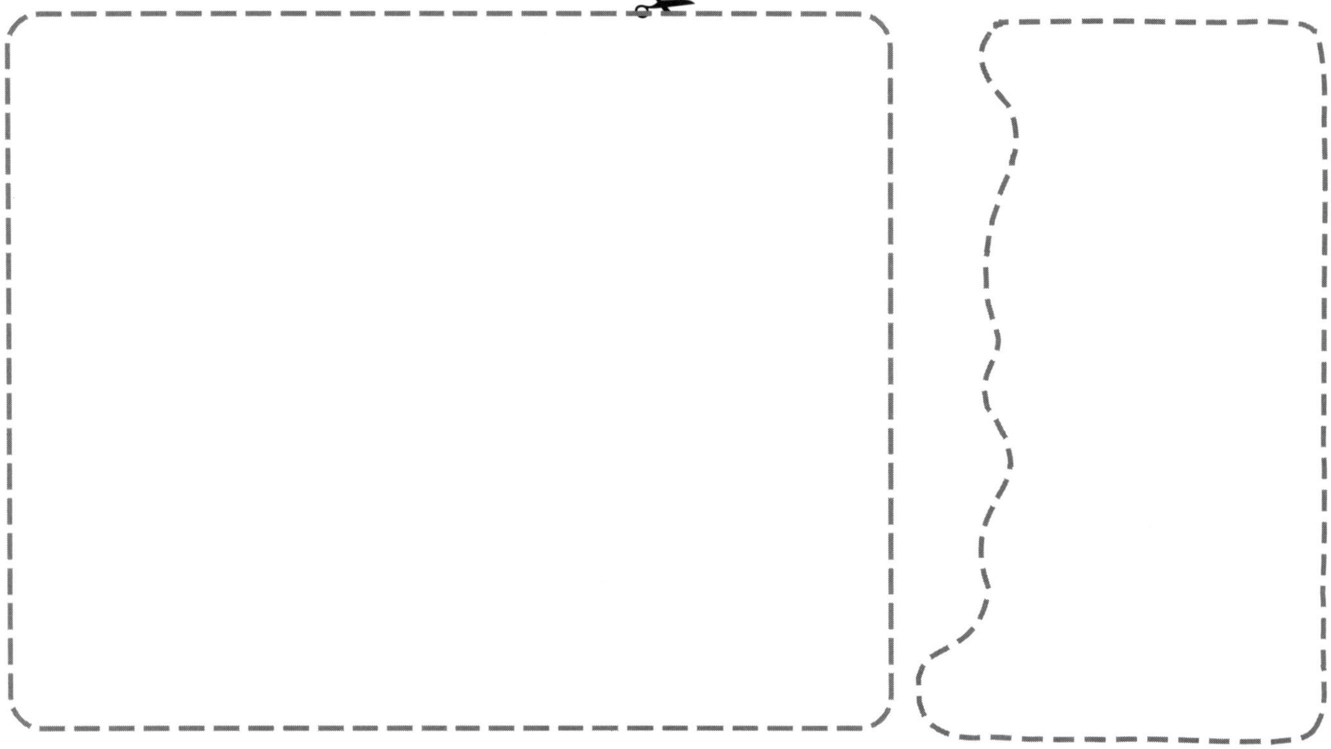

Title Bars

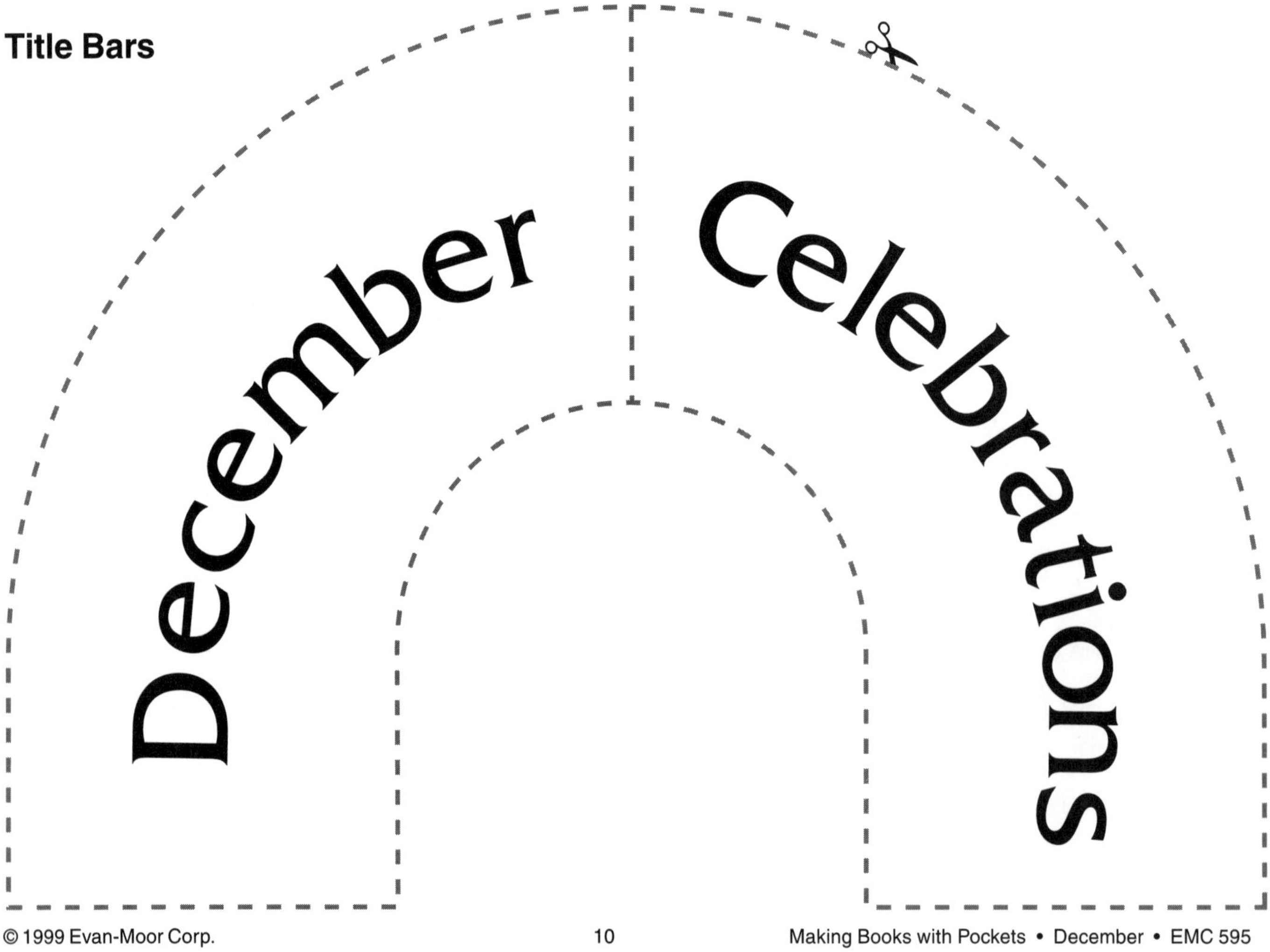

December

Celebrations

Celebrating Las Posadas

A Miniposter

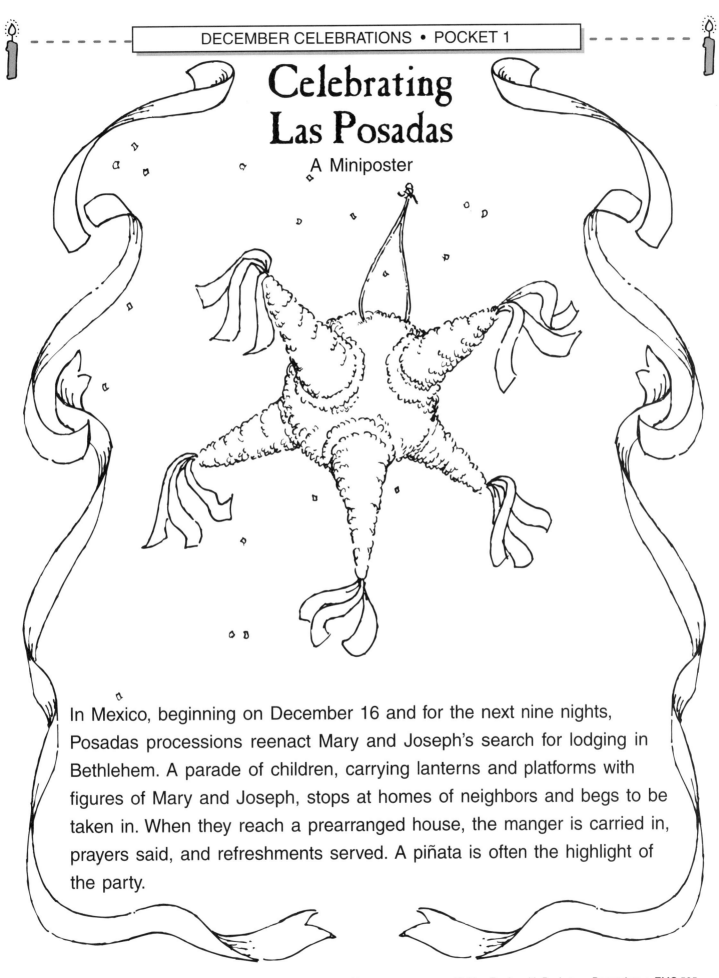

In Mexico, beginning on December 16 and for the next nine nights, Posadas processions reenact Mary and Joseph's search for lodging in Bethlehem. A parade of children, carrying lanterns and platforms with figures of Mary and Joseph, stops at homes of neighbors and begs to be taken in. When they reach a prearranged house, the manger is carried in, prayers said, and refreshments served. A piñata is often the highlight of the party.

In the Stable

Read and discuss several stories about Las Posadas. Ask students if they have ever been in a stable. Talk about the animals that might be found there and what it would be like. Encourage students to "think with their senses"—How would it feel? What would it smell like? How would it sound? Have students imagine spending a night in a stable. Then, have students write about a night spent in a stable.

Materials

- donkey pattern on page 13, reproduced on light brown construction paper for each student
- writing form and lantern on page 14, reproduced for each student
- construction paper
  background—dark blue, 9" x 12" (23 x 30.5 cm)
  stall door—brown, 4" x 12" (10 x 30.5 cm)
  binding strip—brown, 3" x 4" (7.5 x 10 cm)

- gold star stickers
- 3" (7.5 cm) piece of string
- scissors
- glue
- stapler
- tape
- crayons or marking pens

Steps to Follow

1. Cut out the donkey. Glue it to the blue background, leaving the head unglued.

2. Stick gold stars in the sky above the donkey.

3. After students write their stories, cut out the writing forms and staple to the background on the left side only.

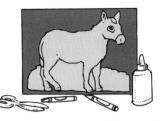

4. Decorate the brown stable door to look like wood. Add a title, such as "In the Stable." Staple it on top of the writing forms.

5. Color, cut out, and fold the lantern. Punch a hole in the top of the lantern. Put the string through the hole. Tape the string under the donkey's mouth. Then glue the donkey's head down.

6. Wrap the binding strip over the stapled edge and glue it down.

Donkey Pattern

13

Writing Form and Lantern

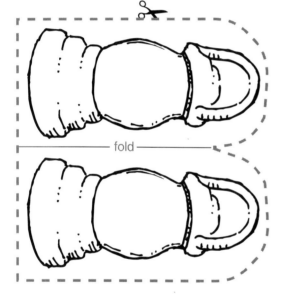

fold

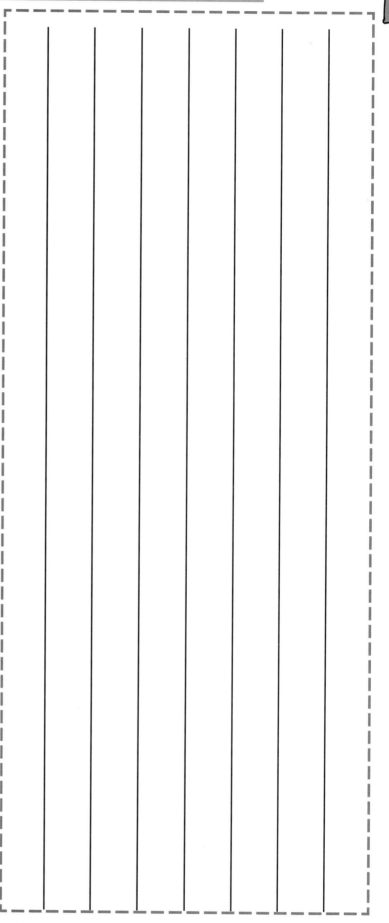

Paper Bag Luminaria

The marchers in the *posada* procession often carry tin lanterns with designs punched in the sides. A candle inside shines through the holes. Create replicas of these luminarias using paper lunch bags.

Write about candles and their light before making the paper bag luminarias. With your class, create a word bank of "light" words. You may want to divide the words into categories—things that make light, ways that light travels, words that tell how bright.

After you have created the list, students should use the words to write free-verse poetry or even one sentence about a candle in the dark. Copy the writing onto the yellow paper to slip inside the paper bag luminaria.

Materials

- paper lunch bag
- hole punch
- yellow construction paper strip, cut to fit inside the lunch bag

Steps to Follow

1. Punch holes in the paper bag using a hole punch. Make the first set along the edges.

2. Then gently fold the bag to make a new set of holes toward the center. Repeat several times.

3. Slip the yellow paper inside the paper bag.

On the night of December 16, celebrate La Posada with a twinkling luminaria. Open the decorated bag, remove the yellow paper, and put about 1" (2.5 cm) of cat litter or sand in the bottom. Then light a votive candle and place it in the bag. Enjoy!

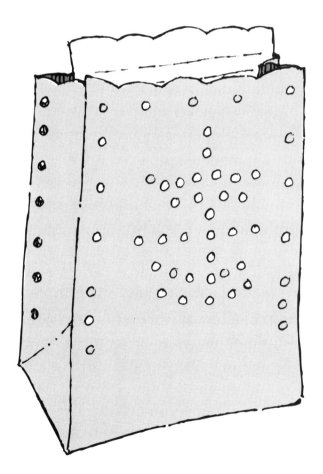

Celebrating Hanukkah
A Miniposter

People celebrate Hanukkah to remember a miracle. Judah, the Maccabee, fought the Syrians for three years. When he and his men finally defeated the Syrians, they reclaimed their temple. The temple was cleaned and the Jewish soldiers relit the Lamp of Eternal Light. They had only enough oil for one day and it would take eight days to get more oil. Incredibly, the oil lasted for eight days.

Hanukkah begins on the twenty-fifth day of the Jewish month of Kislev and it lasts for eight days. During Hanukkah, families gather every night to light the menorah. Traditional foods served during the celebration include potato pancakes, called *latkes*, and applesauce. Children receive small gifts on each of the eight nights and play with a square-sided top called a *dreidel*.

Making a Menorah

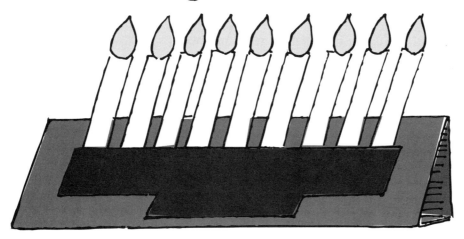

The Hanukkah menorah is a special candleholder. It holds nine candles, one for each of the eight days of Hanukkah and one called the *shammas*, or servant candle. The shammas is used to light the other candles.

Materials

- construction paper
  background—blue, 12" x 18" (30.5 x 45.5 cm)
  candles—nine white, 4" x 1" (10 x 2.5 cm) strips
  flames—nine yellow, 2" x 1" (5 x 2.5 cm) strips
  menorah—black, 11" x 2" (28 x 5 cm)
  base of menorah—black, 6" x 1" (15 x 2.5 cm)

- glue

- scissors

- tape

Steps to Follow

1. Fold the blue paper in half.

2. Fold each long side to form a base.

3. Build the menorah from the bottom up:
   - The small black piece will be the base.
   - The large black piece will be the candleholder.
   - The white strips will be the candles. Glue down the middle candle first. Then lay four candles on either side. Check the spacing before gluing the candles in place.
   - Cut yellow flames and glue them to the top of the candles.

4. Paper clip the base together to make the menorah stand up. Remove the paper clip and fold the menorah flat to fit it in the pocket.

Dreidel

During the Hanukkah celebration, children play a game of chance with a four-sided top called a *dreidel*. Each side has a single Hebrew letter. The letters have a double meaning. They stand for a phrase that means, "A great miracle happened there." They also stand for Yiddish words that give rules for a game.

Purchase a dreidel from a party supply store. Teach the rules of the game and then play it.

Objective: The game is officially over when one player has all the tokens. In the classroom, you may want to replenish a player's token supply when it runs out.

You need: 1 dreidel, 1 cup, and a bag of peanuts, pretzels, or raisins

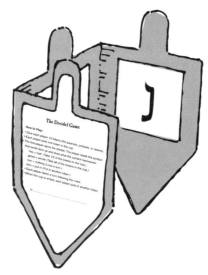

Materials

- dreidel game directions pattern and Hebrew letters on pages 19 and 20, reproduced for each student
- 12" x 18" (30.5 x 45.5 cm) construction paper
- glue
- scissors
- crayons or marking pens

Steps to Follow

1. Fold the construction paper into thirds.

2. Cut out the dreidel game directions pattern. Glue it to the paper. Cut around the top and bottom edges. Do not cut the sides.

3. Open the first flap of the book and glue down the first two Hebrew letters. Open the other flap and glue down the remaining two Hebrew letters.

Dreidel Pattern

The Dreidel Game

How to Play:

• Give each player 10 tokens (the peanuts, pretzels, or raisins).

• Each player puts one token in the cup.

• The first player spins the dreidel. The player reads the symbol that lands face up and does what the symbol represents:

   hey = half (Take ½ of the tokens in the cup.)

   gimel = everything (Take all of the tokens in the cup.)

   nun = nothing (Lose a turn.)

   shin = put in (Put in another token.)

• Each player takes a turn.

• When the cup is empty, each player puts in another token.

by: _____

Dreidel Pattern

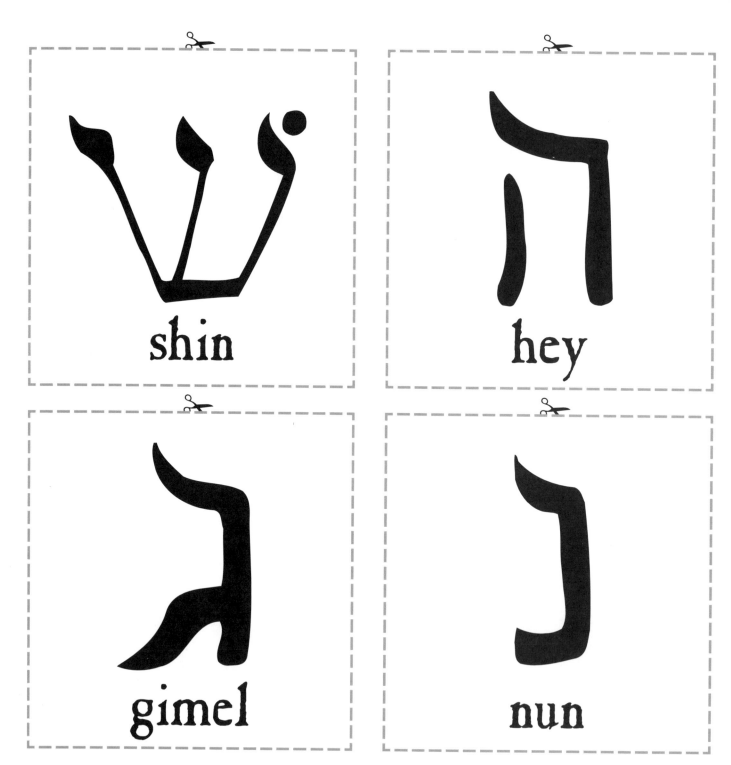

Potato Latkes

Enjoy a latke feast as you read several tales of Hanukkah. Be sure to include the Caldecott winner, *Hershel and the Hanukkah Goblins* by Eric A. Kimmel.

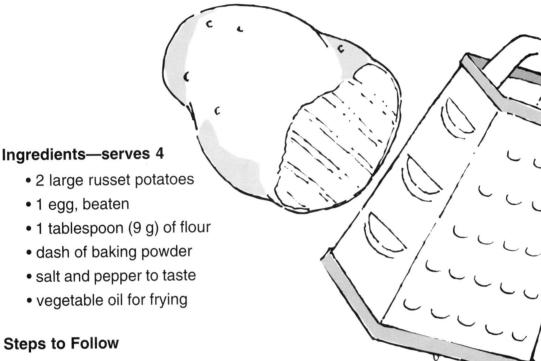

Ingredients—serves 4

- 2 large russet potatoes
- 1 egg, beaten
- 1 tablespoon (9 g) of flour
- dash of baking powder
- salt and pepper to taste
- vegetable oil for frying

Steps to Follow

1. Wash and peel the potatoes.

2. Grate the potatoes with a grater, food processor, or hand-held grater.

3. Drain off the liquid.

4. Add the egg, flour, and baking powder.

5. Heat a small amount of oil in a skillet over medium-high heat until very hot.

6. Carefully spoon potato mixture into oil. Flatten spoonfuls with a spatula.

7. Fry to golden brown on both sides. (This should take about 2 to 3 minutes per side.)

8. Drain on paper towels. Sprinkle with salt and pepper.

9. Serve with applesauce or sour cream.

Celebrating Christmas
A Miniposter

Christmas is a celebration of the birth of Jesus. On December 25, Christians around the world celebrate His birth with the giving of gifts, singing of carols, and family gatherings. Around the world, traditions of Christmas gift-giving vary. In Spain, children believe that three wise men bring them gifts. In Russia, a good witch named Babouska sneaks into houses to slip gifts under children's pillows. Swedish children wait for Jultomten, a present-giving elf, while German children place baskets by their front doors so that the Christkindl will fill them with cookies and candy. American children hang stockings by the chimney on Christmas Eve, hoping for a visit from Santa Claus. In England, Santa is called Father Christmas. Polish children wait for the Star Man, and in France Pere Noel brings presents to children on Christmas Day.

Rudolph the Red-Nosed Reindeer

Rudolph the Red-Nosed Reindeer has become a symbol of the Christmas celebration, as well as the idea that everyone has a special gift. Rudolph had a wonderful shining nose that helped Santa to find his way on Christmas Eve. Make this Rudolph and then have students think about what special gifts they have.

Materials

- construction paper
  head—light brown, 7" (18 cm) square
  ears—light brown, two 2" x 3" (5 x 7.5 cm)
  antlers—dark brown, 9" x 12" (23 x 30.5 cm)
  eyes—white, 2" x 3" (5 x 7.5 cm)
        black, 1" x 2" (2.5 x 5 cm)
  nose—red, 2" (5 cm) square
- black marking pen
- 24" (61 cm) Christmas ribbon
  (about 1" [2.5 cm] wide)
- scissors
- glue

ears

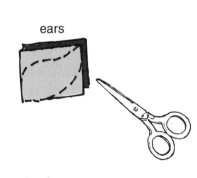

Steps to Follow

1. Hold the two small light brown papers together. Cut two ears as shown. Glue the ears to the head.

2. Trace both hands on the dark brown paper. (Students will need a partner to hold the paper steady.) Cut out the hands and glue them in back of the ears for antlers.

3. Fold the white rectangle in half and cut to make two eyes. Glue to the face. Repeat with the black rectangle to make pupils.

4. Round the corners on the red square to make a nose. Glue to the face.

5. Add a mouth and eyebrows with the black marking pen.

6. Tie the ribbon in a bow and glue it to the bottom of the head.

Four Christmas Stories

Share Christmas stories with students. Then have them write four different stories of their own using the story starters below or story starters that you provide.

Story Starters
The best present I ever received was....
I heard a strange noise coming from under the tree...
This year I hope Santa remembers...
My Christmas Wish

Materials for Package-Shaped Book

- construction paper
  box—12" x 18" (30.5 x 45.5 cm)
  ribbon—two 12" x 1" (30.5 x 2.5 cm) strips
  tag—white, 2" x 3" (5 x 7.5 cm)
- writing paper, cut into 4" x 11" (10 x 28 cm) strips
- glue
- scissors

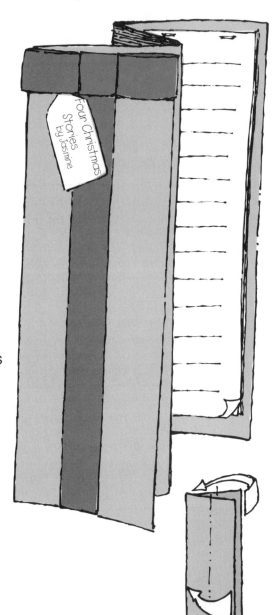

Steps to Follow

1. Accordion fold the large construction paper.

2. Glue one ribbon strip down the center of the front.

3. Make a bow with the second ribbon strip:
   - Cut a square off the end of the strip.
   - Fold both ends to the center.
   - Glue the square on top to hold the ends in place.

4. Glue the bow to the top of the package.

5. Cut a gift tag from the white paper. Write "Four Christmas Stories" and the student's name on the tag and glue it under the bow.

6. Staple all the strips for a single story to one inside section of the package.

Four Christmas
Stories
by Jasmine

A 3-D Christmas Tree
Words That Describe Christmas

The people of Germany and Scandinavia were the first to bring Christmas trees into their homes. In Sweden, many children make straw billy goats and place them under the tree so that evil spirits won't steal the decorations. Most Christmas trees in the United States are grown on Christmas tree farms and shipped to retailers. It takes about eight years to grow an average-size tree.

Before making this three-dimensional Christmas tree for the pocket book, talk with your students about the feelings they see portrayed in the Christmas stories you have shared. List the words in a word bank.

hope	love	faith
joy	peace	charity
compassion	trust	caring
happiness	friendship	

Materials

- tree pattern on page 26, reproduced on green construction paper for each student
- scraps of colored construction paper
- self-adhesive stars
- three 2½" x 1" (6 x 2.5 cm) white strips
- scissors
- hole punch
- glue
- paper clips

Steps to Follow

1. Cut out the tree pattern. Fold on the fold lines.

2. Stick stars on the tree at the "x"s.

3. Punch out holes in colored paper scraps. Glue these circles to the trees as decorations.

4. Choose three words from the "feelings" word bank. Write the words on the white strips.

5. Glue the strips onto the trees.

6. Use the paper clip to hold the tree together so that it stands up, or lay it flat to fit in the pocket.

3-D Tree Pattern

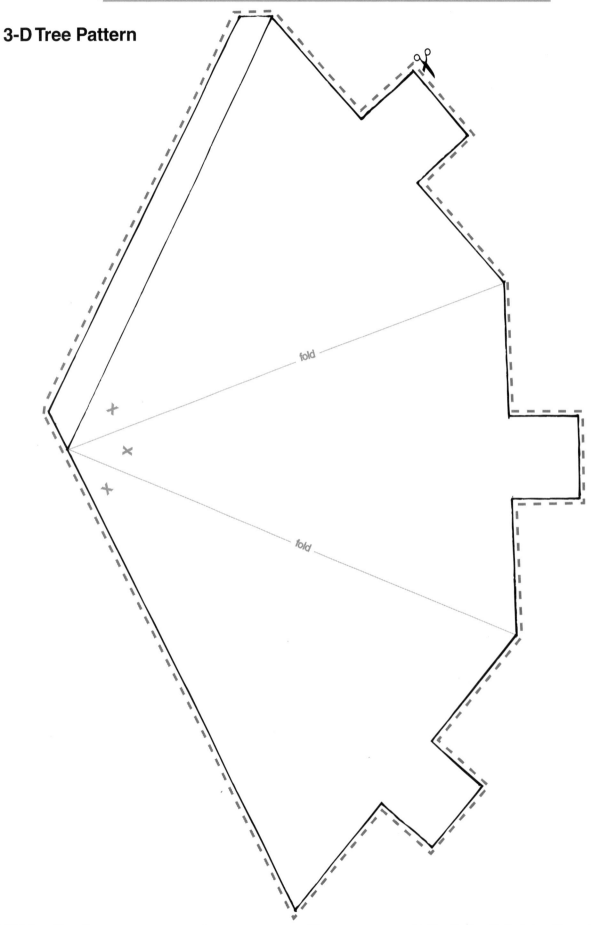

fold

fold

Candy Canes

Sweets are a part of the Christmas celebration. Everyone has their favorite. Make these candy canes after you discuss your students' favorite Christmas treats.

Materials

- white paper squares (any size)
- red crayons or marking pens
- pencils
- 6" (15 cm) piece of red yarn

Steps to Follow

1. Color a red stripe down two touching sides.

2. Turn the paper over. Roll it around a pencil, beginning at a white corner.

3. Curl one end over.

4. Add a bow.

5. Make several candy canes using different-sized squares.

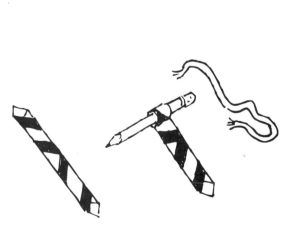

Celebrating Kwanzaa

A Miniposter

Kwanzaa is a Swahili word that means *first fruits*. This holiday was begun in 1966 to celebrate African-American heritage. Families celebrate Kwanzaa for seven days. They light candles in a special candleholder called a *kinara*. Each day of Kwanzaa has a special meaning or principle. At the end of the seven days, children receive handmade gifts. Families and friends enjoy a feast, sing songs, play music, and share stories of their heritage.

A Seven Candles Booklet

The Seven Principles of Kwanzaa are the *Nguzo Saba*. Read about Kwanzaa and talk about the seven principles. Be sure to connect the principles to real experiences. Have your students write a simple description or definition of each principle and give an example of the principle in their lives. Use the descriptions as you make the *mishumaa saba* (seven candles) booklet.

Materials

- page of seven candles on page 30, reproduced for each student
- seven pieces of writing paper, cut 5" x 1" (13 x 2.5 cm)
- book pages, cut from construction paper
  8" x 14" (20 x 35.5 cm)
  8" x 12" (20 x 30.5 cm)
  8" x 10" (20 x 25.5 cm)
  8" x 8" (20 x 20 cm)
  8" x 6" (20 x 15 cm)
  8" x 4" (20 x 10 cm)
  8" x 2" (20 x 5 cm)
- book cover—8" x 14" (20 x 35.5 cm) piece of construction paper
- 2 binder rings
- hole punch
- scissors
- crayons
- glue
- pencils

Steps to Follow

1. Layer the page strips with the left edges even. The shortest strip should be on top. Staple on the left side.

2. Cut out the candles and glue one candle on the right side of each page in order from left to right.

3. Color the center candle black. Color the three candles on the left red and the three candles on the right green.

4. Write the descriptions of the seven principles on the writing paper strips. Glue the strips to the back of each page.

5. Punch holes in all the pages and attach them using the two book rings. Add the title "The Seven Principles of Kwanzaa."

Candle Patterns

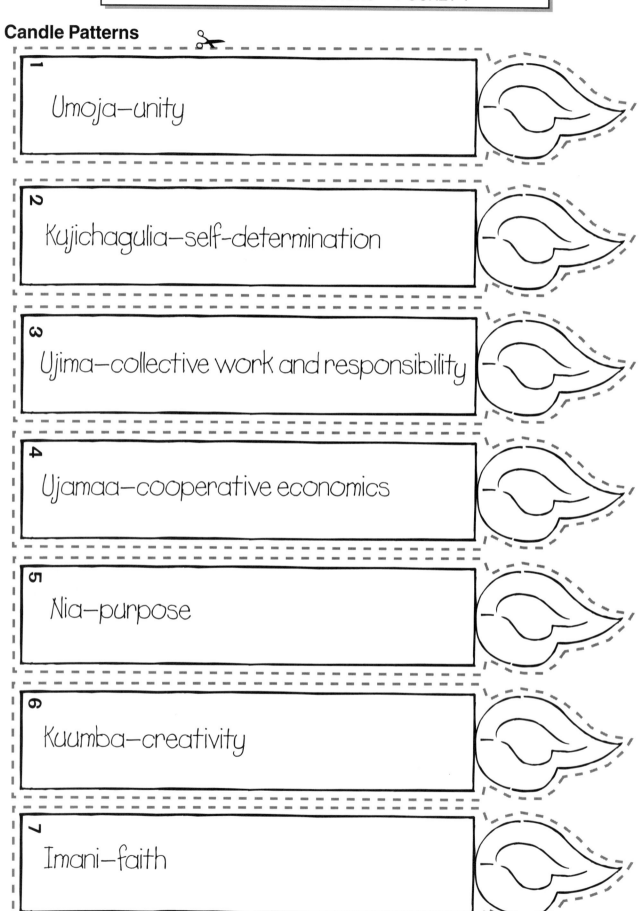

1   Umoja—unity

2   Kujichagulia—self-determination

3   Ujima—collective work and responsibility

4   Ujamaa—cooperative economics

5   Nia—purpose

6   Kuumba—creativity

7   Imani—faith

The Mkeka

A Placemat for Kwanzaa

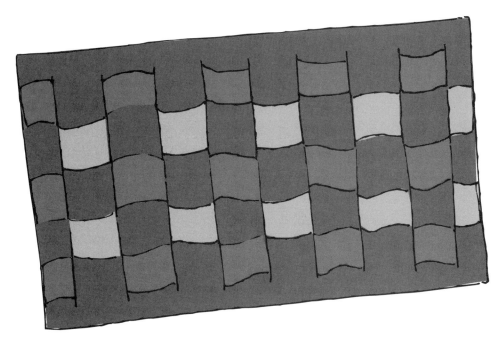

The mkeka is a mat on which the symbols of Kwanzaa are placed. It represents the importance of history and tradition for the African-American family. Make this mkeka for your pocket.

Materials

- construction paper
  mat—black, 12" x 18" (30.5 x 45.5 cm)
  strips—three red and two green, 2" x 18"
    (5 x 45.5 cm)

- scissors

- glue

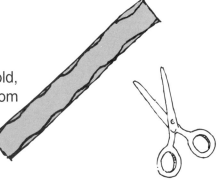

Steps to Follow

1. Fold the black paper in half lengthwise. Starting at the fold, cut strips about 2" (5 cm) apart. Stop about 1" (2.5 cm) from the edge. Do not cut the paper apart.

2. Cut curving edges on the red and green strips.

3. Weave the strips through the black paper. Glue the ends to hold them in place.

       Making Books with Pockets • December • EMC 595

Name: _____

Comparing Candles

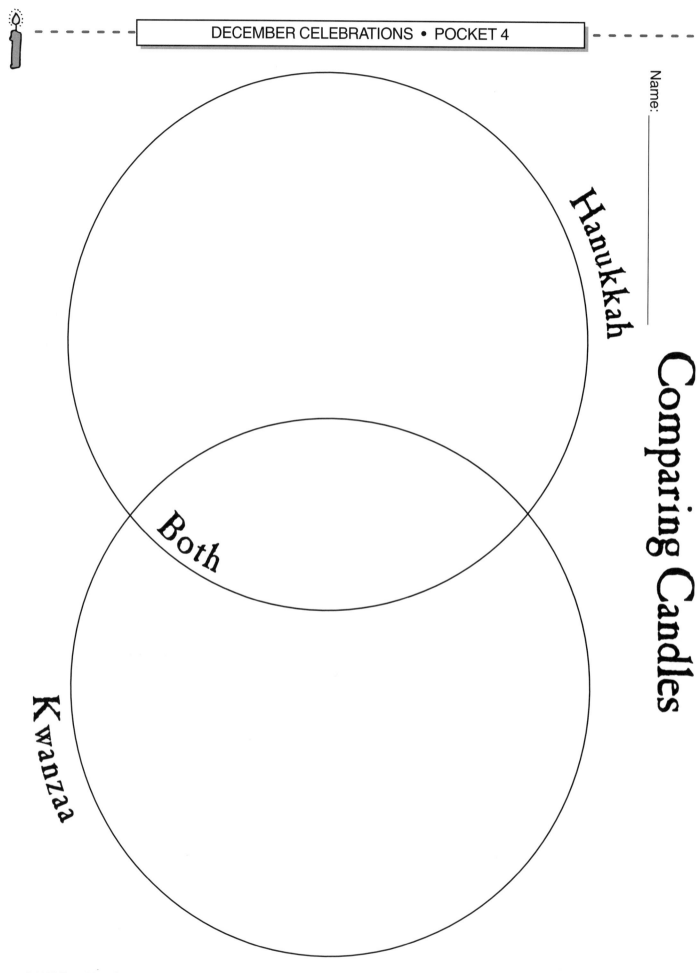

Hanukkah

Both

Kwanzaa

Note: Reproduce this page and page 34 to label each of the four pockets in the December Celebrations book.

Pocket 1

Celebrating La Posada
Candles twinkle along the way
As we look for a place to stay.

Pocket 2

Celebrating Hanukkah
Add one candle every night.
The menorah spreads a special light.

Pocket 3

Celebrating Christmas

The candles are lit. The cooking is done. Carolers are singing. Let's all have some fun.

Pocket 4

Celebrating Kwanzaa

Remember the past and live responsibly today.

The candles in the kinara tell the way.

Hanukkah

hey
gimel
nun
shin
festival of lights
shammas
menorah
oil lamp
dreidel
latkes

Kwanzaa

Mishumaa saba
Nguzo Saba
mkeka
kinara
umoja
kujichagulia
ujamaa
nia
kuumba
imani

La Posada

piñata
nativity scene
procession
Mary and Joseph
Baby Jesus
refreshments
games
dancing
luminarias
lanterns

Christmas

Christmas tree
angels
nativity
wreath
carols
stockings
holly
reindeer
gifts
candy canes

Making Books with Pockets • December • EMC 595

DECEMBER CELEBRATIONS WRITING FORM

Name: ______________________________

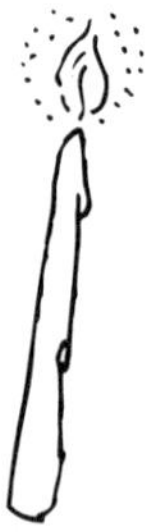

Take It Home

December is a time of vacations as well as celebrations. With your students, make the pocket book cover and three pockets. Add the pocket labels and bind the book together. Reproduce the pocket projects for your students and place them in the appropriate pockets to be taken home and completed during vacation. Students keep a journal of their vacation days, practice important language and math skills, and share their creativity with others. When the New Year begins, students will be eager to share their vacation journals with classmates.

BIBLIOGRAPHY

Amelia's Notebook by Marissa Moss; Tricycle Press, 1995.
Jorah's Journal by Judith Caseley; Greenwillow, 1997.
The Way West: Journal of a Pioneer Woman by Lillian Schlissel; Simon & Schuster, 1993.
Look to the North: A Wolf Pup Diary by Jean Craighead George; Harpercresl, 1997.
My Worst Days Diary by Suzanne Altman; Bantam/Bank Street, 1995.

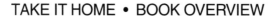
POCKET 1

Journal Writing **pages 40–42**
This vacation journal is a great way to remember special events.

Pencil Toppers **page 43**
Make these terrific toppers for your pencils.

Doorknob Journal Tally **page 44**
Keep track of the times that you remember to write in your vacation journal.

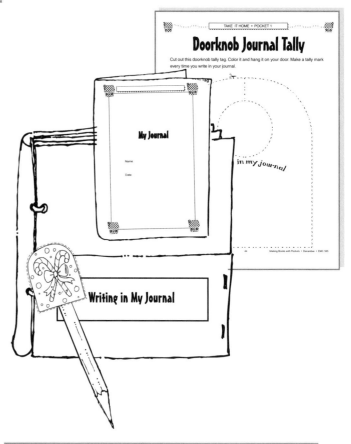

POCKET 2

Reproducible Activities **pages 45–51**
Kids will love these activity pages—dot-to-dot, word search, riddles, and more!

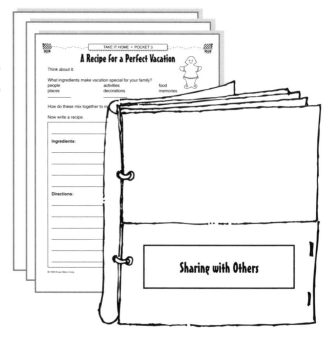

POCKET 3

The Gingerbread House **page 52**
Share this cute cut-and-paste project with a neighbor.

My Candle Card **page 53**
Make this card and send it to a friend as a thank you for lighting up your life.

A Recipe for a Perfect Vacation **page 54**
Appreciate all the ingredients that are blended together to create a pleasant holiday.

Materials

- brown construction paper
  cover—12" (30.5 cm) square
  flap—12" x 9" (30.5 x 23 cm)
  pocket—6" (15 cm) square
  nameplate—3" x 5" (7.5 x 13 cm)
  strap—5" x 2" (13 x 5 cm)
- 4½" x 2½" (11.5 x 6.5 cm) piece
  of laminating film or plastic wrap

- 4½" x 2½" (11.5 x 6.5 cm)
  white paper
- tape
- black crayons or marking pens
- glue
- scissors
- mat knife (for adult use only)

Steps to Follow

1. Round two corners of the pocket. Cut two slits near the top edge for the strap to go through. (An adult may need to do this.) Outline the pocket in black. Glue the pocket to the cover.

2. Gently fold the nameplate in half. Cut out a window. Unfold the nameplate and tape the laminating film in the backside of the window. Write the name on the white paper. Tape the name inside the window. Outline the nameplate in black and glue it to the pocket.

3. Round two corners of the flap and the strap. Outline the strap and the flap in black.

4. Glue the strap to the center of the rounded end of the flap.

5. To judge how the flap should be attached, lay the flap on the pocket and insert the strap in the slip. Fold the flap over the top of the pocket and glue or tape on the backside.

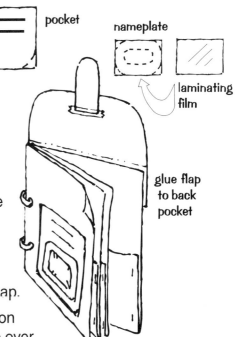

pocket

nameplate

laminating film

glue flap to back pocket

Writing in a Journal

Students make this journal and put it in the pocket. They can record the daily highlights of their vacation.

My Journal

Name: _____

Date: _____

The Importance of Journaling

Read several examples of journals from the bibliography on page 37. Discuss with your students the reasons someone might keep a journal or a diary. Explain that while they are on vacation you would like them to keep a journal. They should write about one thing that happens every day.

Materials

- cover pattern on page 41, reproduced on construction paper for each student
- journal pages on page 42, one page per day for each student
- stapler
- crayons or marking pens

Steps to Follow

1. Cut the pages in half on the cut lines. Decorate the cover and have students write their name on it.

2. Stack the journal pages inside the folded cover.

3. Staple the top of the pages to the back cover.

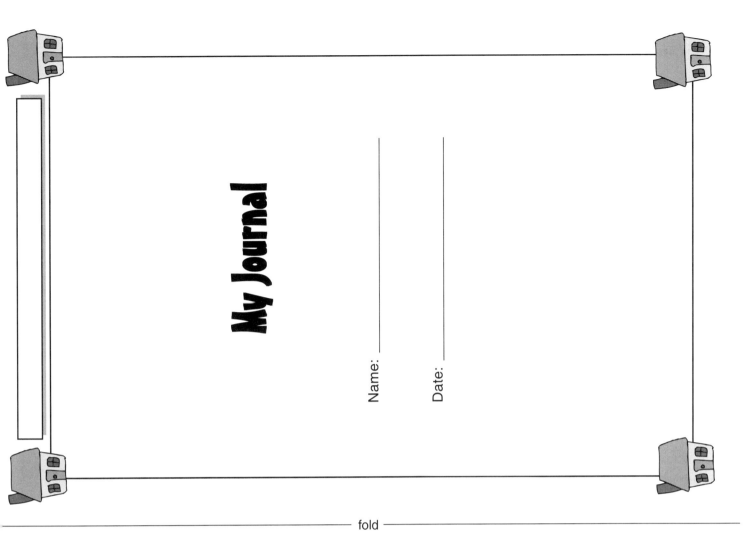

My Journal

Name: _____

Date: _____

fold

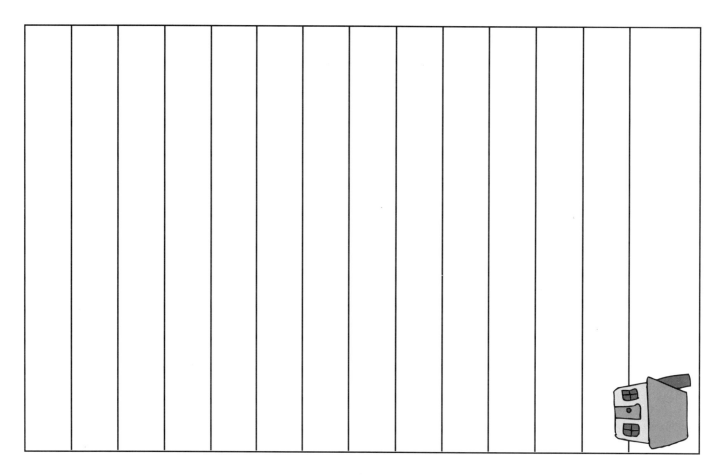

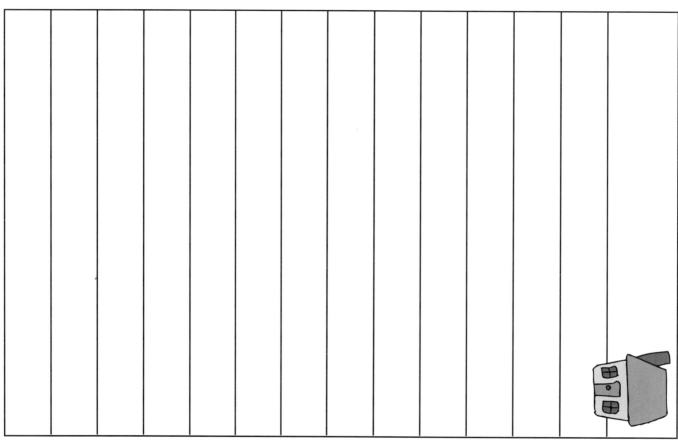

Pencil Toppers

Cut out the pencil toppers. Color them. Cut on the dotted lines. Then decorate your pencils and keep them in your pocket book to use when you write in your journal.

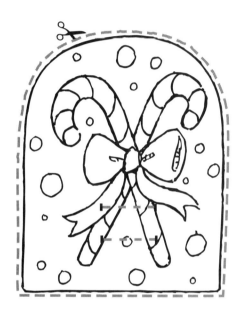

Doorknob Journal Tally

Cut out this doorknob tally tag. Color it and hang it on your door. Make a tally mark every time you write in your journal.

Pattern For Tally Tag

I wrote in my journal

Winter Dot-to-Dot

Connect the dots.
Start at the ☆.

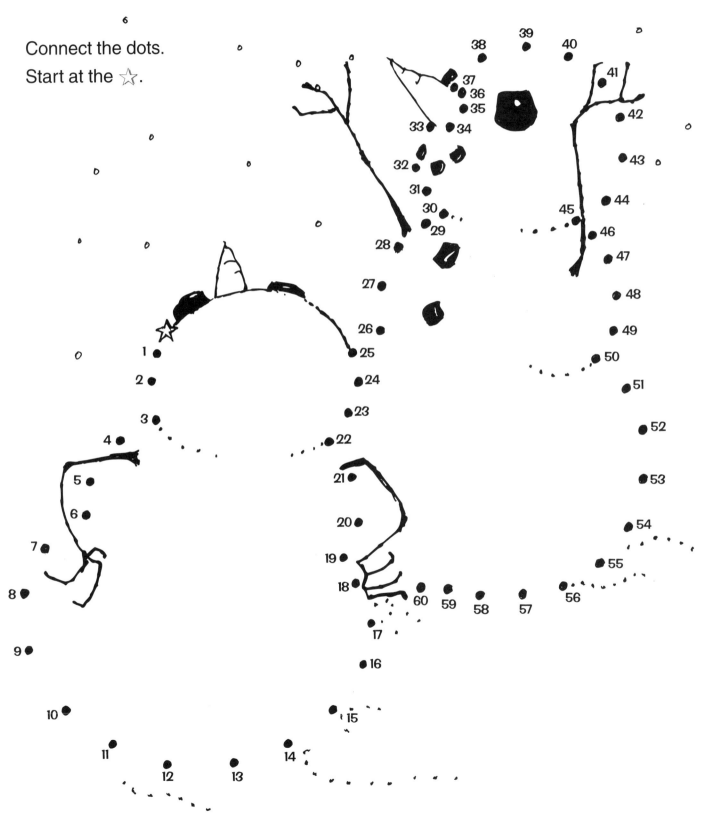

Winter Word Search

Find these winter words.

✓ blizzard	_____ icicle
_____ chilly	_____ mittens
_____ cold	_____ north pole
_____ earmuffs	_____ scarf
_____ freeze	_____ snow
_____ frost	_____ sled
_____ goosebumps	_____ wet
_____ iceberg	_____ wind

g	o	o	s	e	b	u	m	p	s	x	c	m
i	c	i	c	l	e	f	r	o	s	t	o	i
s	n	o	r	t	h	p	o	l	e	w	l	t
n	w	b	l	i	z	z	a	r	d	i	d	t
o	e	e	a	r	m	u	f	f	s	n	s	e
w	t	x	i	c	e	b	e	r	g	d	l	n
f	r	e	e	z	e	s	c	a	r	f	e	s
x	c	h	i	l	l	y	b	e	a	r	d	x

Making Books with Pockets • December • EMC 595

The Relatives Came

Use the clues to complete the crossword puzzle.

Across

4. the father of your mother or father
6. a female parent
8. to go see someone
9. a male parent
11. your aunt's child
12. opposite of sister
14. the mother of your mother or father

Down

1. the brother of your mother or father
2. a girl child
3. a person in your family
5. a boy child
7. opposite of brother
10. the sister of your mother or father
11. not a grown-up
13. to go from one place to another place

Word Box

aunt	father	sister	daughter
brother	grandfather	son	relative
child	grandmother	travel	visit
cousin	mother	uncle	

Winter Mystery Word

Use the picture clues to fill in the words. Then read the mystery word.

1.

2.

3.

4.

5.

6.

7.

The mystery word is _____ .

Draw it here.

What Goes Together?

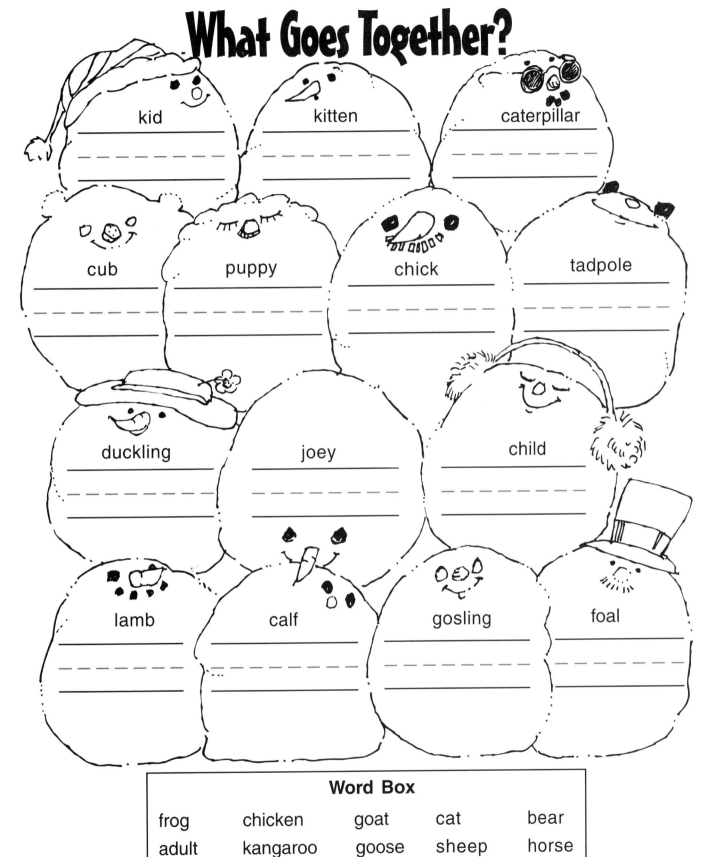

kid

kitten

caterpillar

cub

puppy

chick

tadpole

duckling

joey

child

lamb

calf

gosling

foal

Word Box

frog	chicken	goat	cat	bear
adult	kangaroo	goose	sheep	horse
cow	dog	duck	butterfly	

Mystery Picture

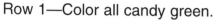

Color the boxes to find the mystery picture.

Row 1—Color all candy green.
Row 2—Color all things you can draw with green.
Row 3—Make everything you put on your feet green.
Row 4—Color everything on your face green.
Row 5—Make things that fly green.
Row 6—Make all fruit green.

Row 7—Color all flowers green.
Row 8—Make all color words green.
Row 9—Color all names green.
Row 10—Color all machines brown.
Row 11—Color plants brown.
Row 12—Color things that you drink blue.

Now color all toys on this page red.

1	milk	tomato	pepper	pie	jelly bean	bread	fish	cake	chicken
2	cloud	rain	thunder	pencil	teddy bear	chalk	wind	snow	sunshine
3	cap	scarf	glove	sock	boot	slipper	dress	shirt	belt
4	toes	knee	nose	sled	chin	eye	lips	finger	arm
5	chair	table	plane	bird	blimp	marble	jet	bed	stool
6	cabbage	banana	lime	grape	pineapple	apple	pear	peach	spinach
7	barn	rose	ball	tulip	daisy	daffodil	jump rope	geranium	shed
8	red	top	yellow	blue	doll	purple	orange	kite	brown
9	Jo Ellen	Anna	Bill	Marilyn	Lucy	Olive	Earl	Ginny	Joy
10	Texas	New York	Idaho	Oregon	tractor	Iowa	Ohio	Utah	Nevada
11	under	over	into	above	fir tree	below	next	after	by
12	elf	fairy	pixie	juice	milk	lemonade	giant	unicorn	ghost

Winter Riddles

Use the code to find the answers.

a–1	e–4	k–7	r–10	u–13
c–2	h–5	n–8	s–11	y–15
d–3	i–6	o–9	t–12	z–16

Where do gingerbread people sleep?

13	8	3	4	10		2	9	9	7	6	4		11	5	4	4	12	11

Why does Rudolph need an umbrella?

5	4	11		1
		,		

10	4	6	8	3	4	4	10

Making Books with Pockets • December • EMC 595

1. Color. 2. Cut. 3. Fold. 4. Paste.
Then give this little gingerbread house to a friend in your neighborhood.

The
Gingerbread
House

TAKE IT HOME • POCKET 3

My Candle Card

This candle card is a great thank you to someone who helps to light up your days.

1. Color.

2. Cut.

3. Fold.

4. Send.

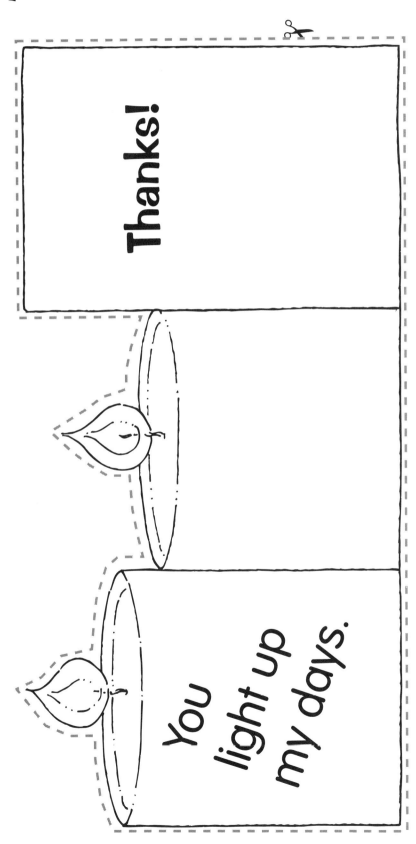

A Recipe for a Perfect Vacation

Think about it:

What ingredients make vacation special for your family?

people   activities   food

places   decorations   memories

_____   _____   _____

How do these mix together to make your vacation fun?

Now write a recipe.

_____'s Recipe for a Perfect Vacation

Ingredients:

_____   _____

_____   _____

_____   _____

Directions:

_____

_____

_____

_____

_____

_____

Note: Reproduce this page to label each of the three pockets in the Take It Home book.

Pocket 1

Writing in My Journal

Pocket 2

Practicing What I've Learned

Pocket 3

Sharing with Others

TAKE IT HOME SPELLING DICTIONARY

A
about
add
after
again
all
along
and
any
anything
are
around
as
ask
at
away

B
back
bank
bath
be
because
bee
been
before
belong
big
birthday
black
blew
boat
boil
bone
book
both
box
boy
bring
brother
brown
but
by

C
cake
call
came
can
candle
candy
card
chain
chase
children
coat
come
cook
could
cute

D
day
did
didn't
do
doing
down
draw
dress
drop

E
each
eat
egg
end

F
fast
father
fawn
find
first
flew
float
fly
for
found
four
fox
friend
from
fun
funny

G
game
gave
get
gifts
girl
give
go
good
got

H
had
hand
happy
has
have
he
help
her
here
him
his
home
hop
hot
house
how
hurt

I
if
in
inside
into
is
it

J
jam
just

K
kind
kite
know

L
land
last
less
letter
like
line
little
live
long
look
love

M
make
man
many
may
mean
men
mine
mix
more
most
mother
much
must
my

N
name
nap
new
nice
no
not
now
number

O
of
off
oil
old
on
one
or
other
out
outside
over

P
pack
paint
part
party
paw
people
pet
place
play
present
pull
puppy
push
put

Q
queen
quick

R
rain
ran
read
red
ride
ring
round
run

S
sack
said
save
saw
say
school
see
send
sent
she
sheep
shook
shop
shout
show
side
silly
sing
sister
slow
small
so
soil
some
soon
stand
star
start
stick
still
stone
stop
store
such
sunny

T
take
tall
tell
than
thank
that
the
their
them
then
there
these
they
thing
think
this
time
to
today
told
too
took
toy
train
treat
tree
trick
trip
try
turn
two

U
under
up
us
use

V
very

W
wait
wall
want
was
water
way
we
well
went
were
what
when
where
which
who
why
will
wish
with
would

Y
yell
yes
you
your

Z
zoo

TAKE IT HOME WRITING FORM

Name: _____

When It's Winter

In cold climates, getting ready for winter is a big thing. For animals and people alike, it's a matter of survival. This pocket book takes a look at the ways some animals respond to the coldest time of the year—hibernation, changing coloration, migration—and how people adapt to the harsh weather conditions that winter brings.

When It's Winter

Book Overview _____ **pages 59 and 60**
These pages show and tell what is in each pocket.

Cover Design _____ **pages 61 and 62**

Pocket Projects _____ **pages 63–86**
Step-by-step directions and patterns for the activities that go in each pocket.

Pocket Labels _____ **pages 87 and 88**

Picture Dictionary _____ **page 89**
Use the picture dictionary to introduce new vocabulary and as a spelling reference. Students can add new pictures, labels, and descriptive adjectives to the page as their vocabulary increases.

Writing Form _____ **page 90**
Use this form for story writing or as a place to record additional vocabulary words.

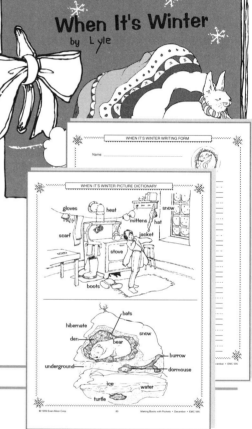

BIBLIOGRAPHY

Animals in Winter by Henrietta Bancroft & Richard G. Van Gelder; HarperCollins Juvenile Books, 1997.

Animals in Winter by Ron Fisher; National Geographic Society, 1996.

Black Bears (Black Bear Magic for Kids) by Jeff Fair; Gareth Stevens, 1991.

A Caribou Journey by Debbie S. Miller; Little, Brown & Co., 1994.

Every Autumn Comes the Bear by Jim Arnosky; Putnam, 1996.

An Extraordinary Life: The Story of a Monarch Butterfly by Laurence Pringle; Orchard Books, 1997.

The Flight of the Snow Geese by Deborah King; Orchard Books, 1998.

Gray Whales by John F. Prevost; Abdo & Daughters. 1996.

How Do Birds Find Their Way? by Roma Gans; HarperCollins, 1996.

Monarch Butterfly by Gail Gibbons; Holiday House, 1989.

Monarchs by Kathryn Lasky; Gulliver Green, 1993.

A Pod of Gray Whales: An Affectionate Portrait by Francios Gohier; Silver Burdett, 1995.

Time to Sleep by Denise Fleming; Henry Holt & Co., 1997.

What Do Animals Do in Winter?: How Animals Survive the Cold by Melvin Berger & Gilda Berger; Ideals Children's Books, 1995.

POCKET 1

**Some Animals
Hibernate in Winter**   **page 63**
Here is a snippet of background information for the teacher.

**Fascinating
Hibernation Facts**   **pages 63 and 64**
Students will enjoy sharing these facts with their families when they take home this pocket book.

**Who's
Hibernating Here?**   **pages 63, 65, and 66**
Match clues and animal pictures to fill the pages of this accordion-fold book.

**My Long
Winter's Nap**   **pages 63 and 67**
In this writing project, students consider what they would do if they had to hibernate.

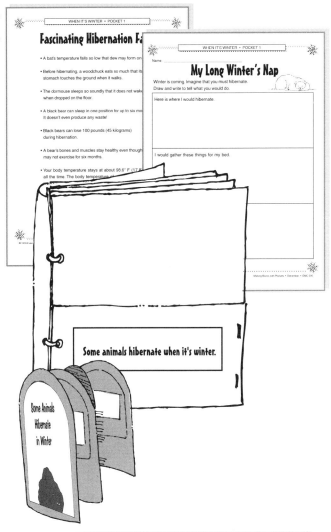

POCKET 2

**Some Animals Change
Color in Winter**   **page 68**
Introductory information for the teacher.

**Arctic Animals
Flip Book**   **pages 69 and 70**
Flip open the pages to read about four different animals that change color in the winter.

**Wintering Over in
Our Classroom**   **pages 71 and 72**
What kind of coloration would a shy little animal from outer space need to live unnoticed in your classroom? Students explore this question by writing and drawing.

POCKET 3

**The Monarch
Butterfly Migrates
to Warmer Places** **pages 73–75**
Learn about monarch migration with this
pull-through project.

**The California
Gray Whale Migrates
to Warmer Waters** **pages 76–78**
Students record important information about
the gray whale migration in the form of a flip
book.

**Snow Geese Fly
South for the Winter** **pages 79–81**
Students follow directions to trace the
migration route of snow geese on a map.

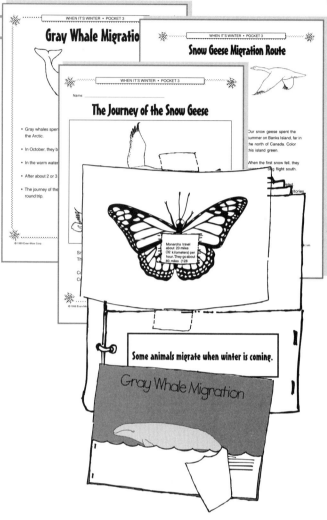

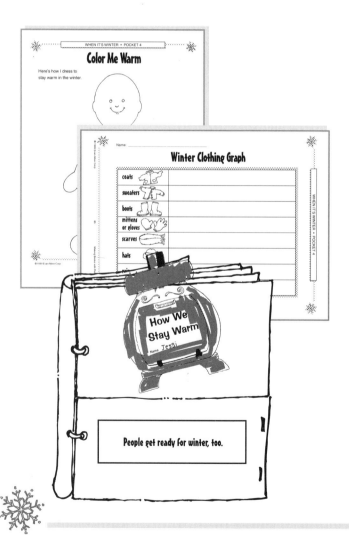

POCKET 4

**How We Stay
Warm Shape Book** **pages 82–84**
A pot-bellied stove holds student writing
about how we stay warm in cold weather.

**Winter
Clothing Graph** **pages 82 and 85**
After sorting winter clothing items from the
class coat rack, graph the results.

Color Me Warm **pages 82 and 86**
Dress a paper doll to show how you stay
warm in the winter.

Materials

- background—blue, 12" (30.5 cm) square construction paper
- pattern for stocking cap and rabbit on page 62, reproduced on white construction paper for each student
- crayons or marking pens
- scissors
- glue
- toothpicks
- white glitter

Steps to Follow

1. Color the stocking cap using bright colors and cut it out.

2. Color and cut out the rabbit.

3. Position the cap and the rabbit on the background paper so that the rabbit's ears are on top of the cap. Glue in place.

4. Use toothpicks to draw snowflakes and a ground line with glue.

5. Sprinkle white glitter on the glue. When the glitter dries, dump off the excess.

Cover Patterns

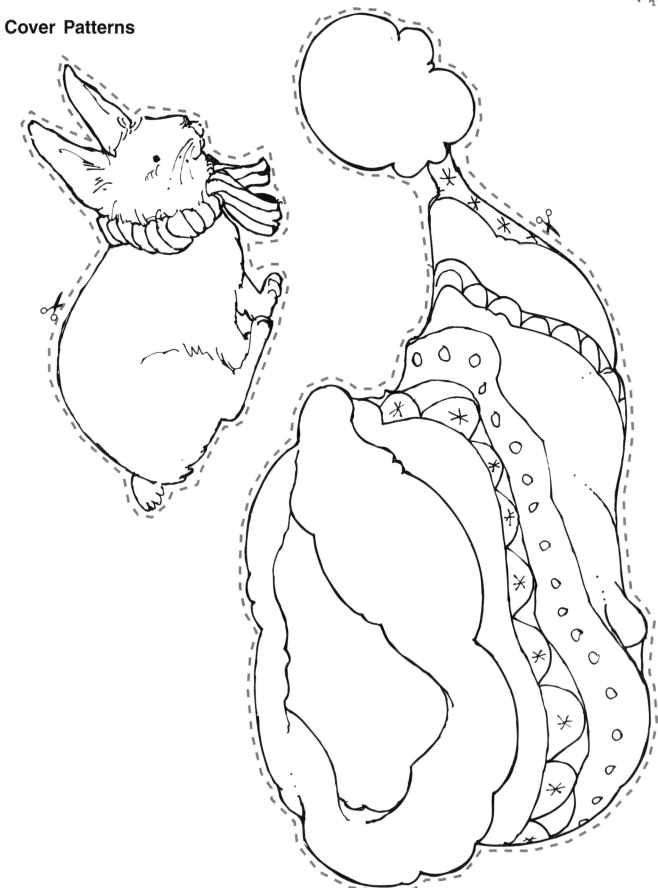

Some Animals Hibernate in Winter

Sleeping very deeply through the winter is called *hibernation*. Lack of available food is what makes some warm-blooded animals hibernate. Before they go to sleep, they stuff themselves with food to build up fat reserves that provide energy during hibernation.

Cold-blooded animals, such as snakes, frogs, and turtles, have bodies that are the same temperature as their surroundings. So they hibernate to keep from freezing to death.

During hibernation, an animal's body becomes very chilled. Its heartbeat slows down so that hardly any energy is used.

Fascinating Hibernation Facts

After reading appropriate information about hibernation, reproduce the information on page 64 for each student. They will love to share the facts with their families when they take this pocket book home.

Who's Hibernating Here?

Materials

- hibernating animals clues on page 65, reproduced for each student
- animal pictures and cover form on page 66, reproduced for each student
- 6" x 18" (15 x 45.5 cm) brown construction paper
- scissors
- glue
- pencils
- marking pens

Steps to Follow

1. Accordion-fold the brown paper.

2. Cut out the cover form and glue it to the front. Round the top corners of the brown paper.

3. Cut out the clues and glue one to each inside page.

4. Cut out the animal pictures and glue each one on the correct page.

My Long Winter's Nap

What if you had to hibernate? How would you get ready? Where would you go? There are a lot of details to consider.

Use the writing form on page 67 for students to plan their "hibernation."

Fascinating Hibernation Facts

- A bat's temperature falls so low that dew may form on its fur.

- Before hibernating, a woodchuck eats so much that its stomach touches the ground when it walks.

- The dormouse sleeps so soundly that it does not wake even when dropped on the floor.

- A black bear can sleep in one position for up to six months. It doesn't even produce any waste!

- Black bears can lose 100 pounds (45 kilograms) during hibernation.

- A bear's bones and muscles stay healthy even though they may not exercise for six months.

- Your body temperature stays at about 98.6° F (17.8° C) all the time. The body temperature of a hibernating woodchuck is about 50° F (10° C).

Hibernating Clues

paste

I sleep so soundly that I will
not wake up if you touch me.

paste

I find a dry cave and hibernate
hanging from the roof.

paste

I am hibernating in the mud
at the edge of the pond.

paste

My den can be many places—under
a log or in a cave.

Book Cover and Animal Pictures

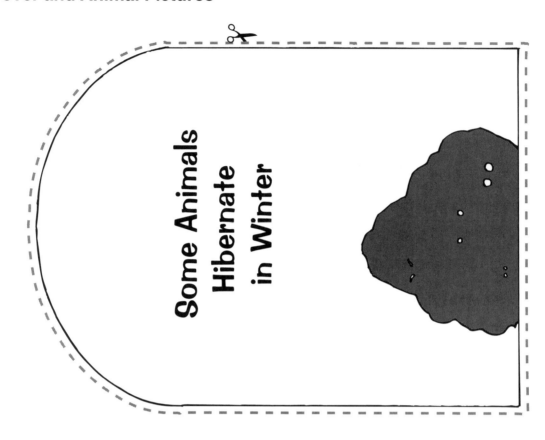

Some Animals Hibernate in Winter

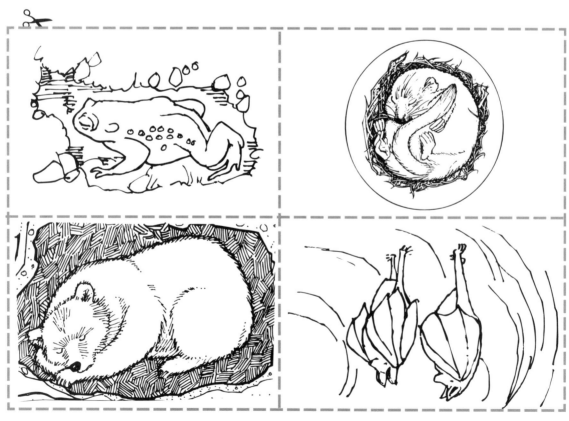

Name: _____

My Long Winter's Nap

Winter is coming. Imagine that you must hibernate.
Draw and write to tell what you would do.

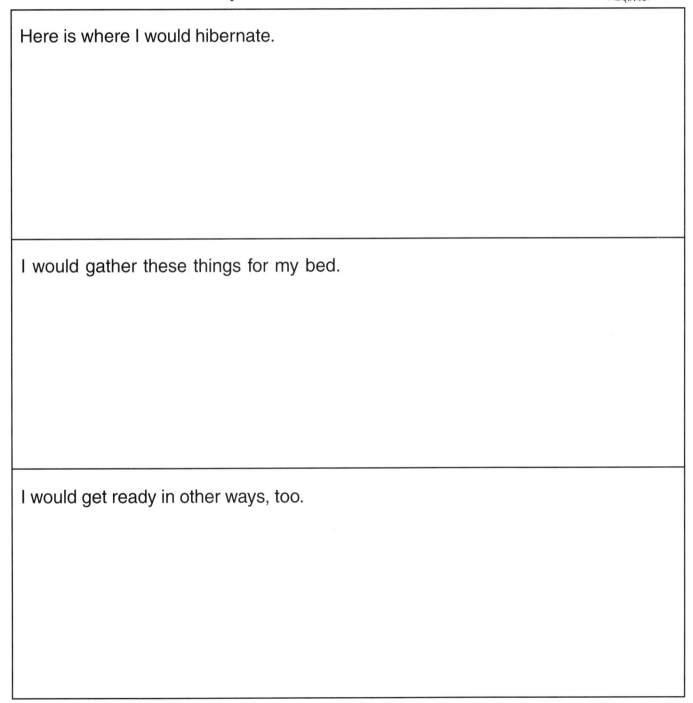

Here is where I would hibernate.

I would gather these things for my bed.

I would get ready in other ways, too.

Some Animals Change Color in Winter

Many arctic animals do not hibernate. They must find food and keep from being eaten in the winter as well as in the summer. To survive in a cold, white landscape, many arctic animals change color. Ermines, arctic foxes, arctic hares, and ptarmigans are brown during the summer. In winter they turn white so that they can move about unseen.

Arctic Animals Flip Book

Materials

- animal patterns on page 69, reproduced for each student
- animal information on page 70, reproduced for each student
- 6" x 12" (15 x 30.5 cm) construction paper, 4 per student
- scissors
- glue
- hole punch
- small binder rings or yarn

Steps to Follow

1. Read the information sheet together. Then color the animal pictures to show each animal in the summer and in the winter. Cut out the pictures.

2. Fold over one-third on the right end of each piece of construction paper.

3. Glue both pictures of an animal to the folded end and cut to make two flaps.

4. Write the animal's name on the left side of the paper.

5. Cut out the animal information and glue each piece behind the correct picture.

6. Put all four "flip pages" together. Punch a hole in the top left corner and use a binder ring or yarn to hold the book together.

Wintering Over in Our Classroom

Reproduce pages 71 and 72 for each student. Then pose this imaginary situation:

> "A strange little animal from outer space must spend this winter in our classroom until its ship is able to come for it in the spring. Naturally, it doesn't want to be seen, so it must change its coloration to blend in."

Challenge students to color the pattern so that the animal can stay somewhere in the classroom without being seen.

Write about how this animal will spend its time in your class.

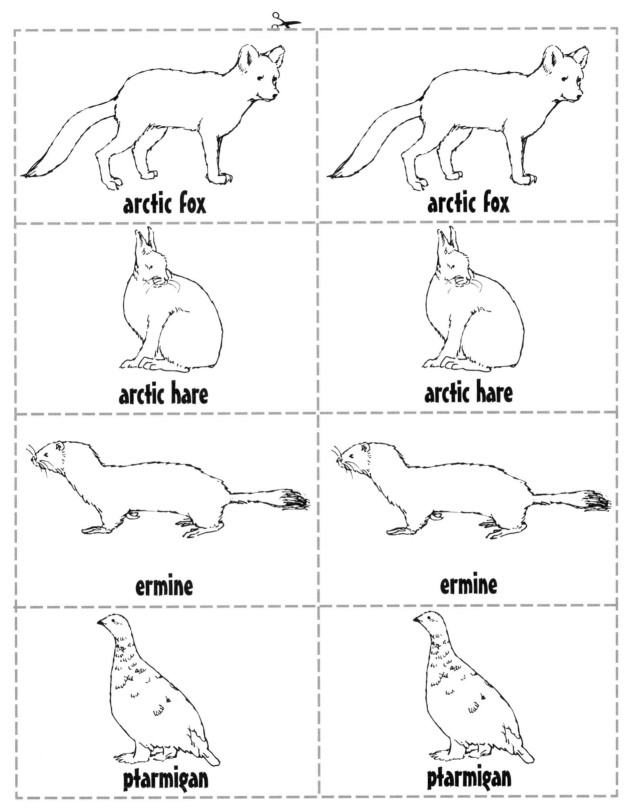

arctic fox

arctic fox

arctic hare

arctic hare

ermine

ermine

ptarmigan

ptarmigan

In the spring, the ptarmigan's feathers are brown and yellow like the grasses of the tundra.

In the winter, the ptarmigan is almost all white. At night, it digs a burrow in the snow to sleep.

The arctic hare's thick winter coat is pure white. A hundred or more hares crowd together for warmth and protection.

In summer, the arctic hare eats many kinds of plants. It's brown fur matches the tundra.

The arctic fox's fur is very thick and oily, so it sheds water. In the winter, the fox's white fur blends in with the snow.

The coats of arctic foxes are reddish brown in the summer.

In the winter, the coat of the ermine turns white except for a black tip on its tail.

Short dark-brown hair covers the ermine in the summer.

Name: _____

Wintering Over in Our Classroom

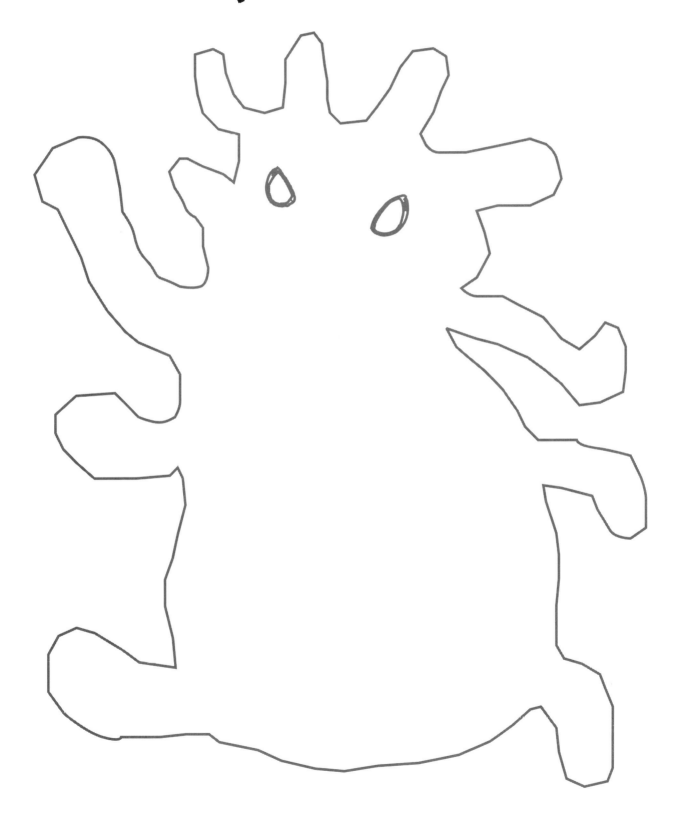

Name: _____

My Winter in Room _____

_____

_____

_____

_____

_____

_____

_____

_____

_____

_____

_____

_____

_____

The Monarch Butterfly Migrates to Warmer Places

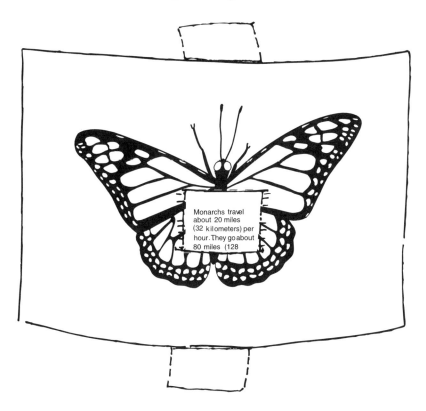

Monarchs travel about 20 miles (32 kilometers) per hour. They go about 80 miles (128

Read one or more of the many excellent books on this insect traveler. Make this monarch with information on a pull-through strip to reinforce what was learned.

Materials

- monarch butterfly pattern on page 74, reproduced for each student
- monarch butterfly information on page 75, reproduced for each student
- orange marking pens or crayons
- scissors
- mat knife (for adult use only)

Steps to Follow

1. Students color the large areas on the butterfly's wings orange. Use photos in reference books as guides.

2. Have an adult use a mat knife to cut the two slits on the butterfly.

3. Cut out the information strip and thread it through the slits in the butterfly.

4. Read the information about monarch butterfly migration together.

Name: _____

In late summer, monarch butterflies leave the northern United States and Canada and begin their flight south.

Butterflies from east of the Rocky Mountains fly to Mexico. Butterflies from west of the Rocky Mountains fly to California.

Monarchs travel about 20 miles (32 kilometers) per hour. They go about 80 miles (128 kilometers) a day. They can not fly if it gets colder than 55° F (13° C).

When winter is over, the monarchs begin the journey north. On the way, new generations of butterflies will be born. The third generation of butterflies will arrive at the summer homes.

In late summer, monarch butterflies leave the northern United States and Canada and begin their flight south.

Butterflies from east of the Rocky Mountains fly to Mexico. Butterflies from west of the Rocky Mountains fly to California.

Monarchs travel about 20 miles (32 kilometers) per hour. They go about 80 miles (128 kilometers) a day. They can not fly if it gets colder than 55° F (13° C).

When winter is over, the monarchs begin the journey north. On the way, new generations of butterflies will be born. The third generation of butterflies will arrive at the summer homes.

In late summer, monarch butterflies leave the northern United States and Canada and begin their flight south.

Butterflies from east of the Rocky Mountains fly to Mexico. Butterflies from west of the Rocky Mountains fly to California.

Monarchs travel about 20 miles (32 kilometers) per hour. They go about 80 miles (128 kilometers) a day. They can not fly if it gets colder than 55° F (13° C).

When winter is over, the monarchs begin the journey north. On the way, new generations of butterflies will be born. The third generation of butterflies will arrive at the summer homes.

The California Gray Whale Migrates to Warmer Waters

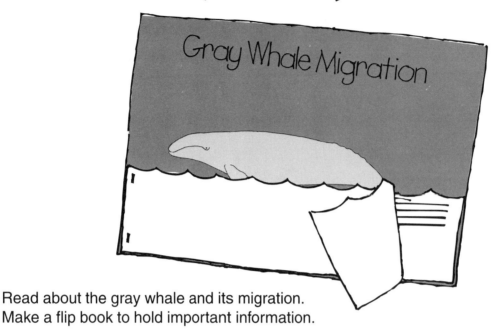

Read about the gray whale and its migration.
Make a flip book to hold important information.

Materials

- gray whale migration pattern on page 77, reproduced on gray paper for each student
- gray whale facts on page 78, reproduced on a transparency (optional)
- construction paper
  background—blue, 9" x 12" (23 x 30.5 cm)
  waves for facts—white, 4½" x 12" (11.5 x 30.5 cm), several per student
- scissors
- crayons
- glue
- black marking pens
- stapler

Steps to Follow

1. Color and cut out the gray whale pattern. Glue it to the middle of the blue paper.

2. Using black marking pen, write "Gray Whale Migration" across the top of the paper.

3. Use your readings to generate facts about gray whale migration, or use the transparency made from page 78.

4. Instruct students to write one fact about gray whale migration on each piece of white paper.

5. Stack the papers together and cut "waves" along the top edge. Add a "cover" wave.

6. Staple the facts to the background along the left side.

Gray Whale Pattern

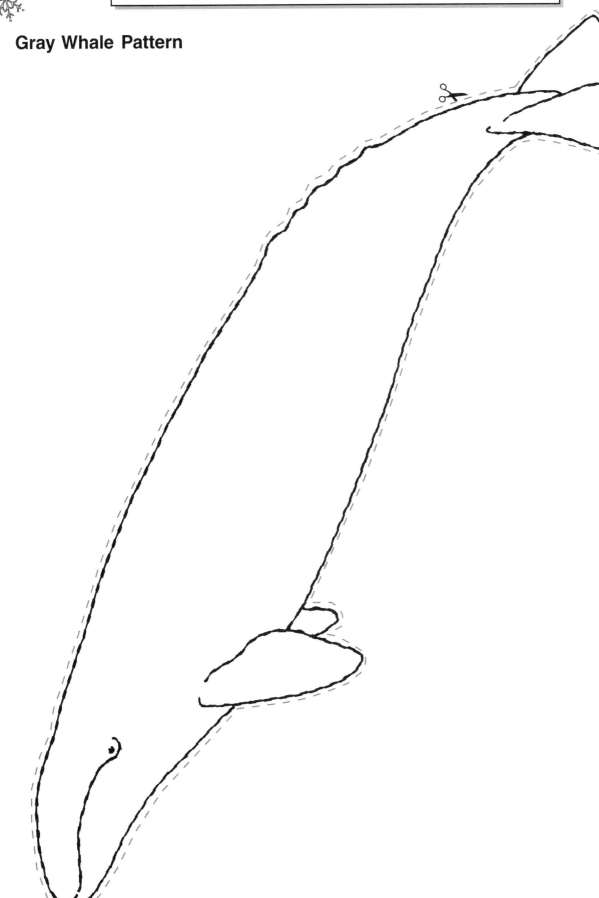

Gray Whale Migration

- Gray whales spend the summer feeding in the Bering and Chukchi Seas in the Arctic.

- In October, they begin the long 2-to-3-month trip to Baja California, Mexico.

- In the warm waters of Mexico, whale calves are born.

- After about 2 or 3 months, the whales begin to travel north again.

- The journey of the gray whale is about 10,000 miles (16,000 kilometers) round trip.

Snow Geese Fly South for the Winter

There are several populations of snow geese that nest in the arctic from Siberia, Russia, to Baffin Island, Canada. They migrate to wintering areas in the southern United States and Mexico. This lesson focuses on the population of lesser snow geese that nest in the western Canadian Arctic and migrates to Colorado, New Mexico, and Mexico.

Materials

- snow goose cover sheet on page 80, reproduced for each student
- migration map on page 81, reproduced for each student and made into a transparency, if desired
- crayons
- stapler
- pencils

Steps to Follow

1. Follow the directions on the map to trace the migration route of the snow geese.

2. Color the cover sheet and staple it to the map.

Name: _____

The Journey of the Snow Geese

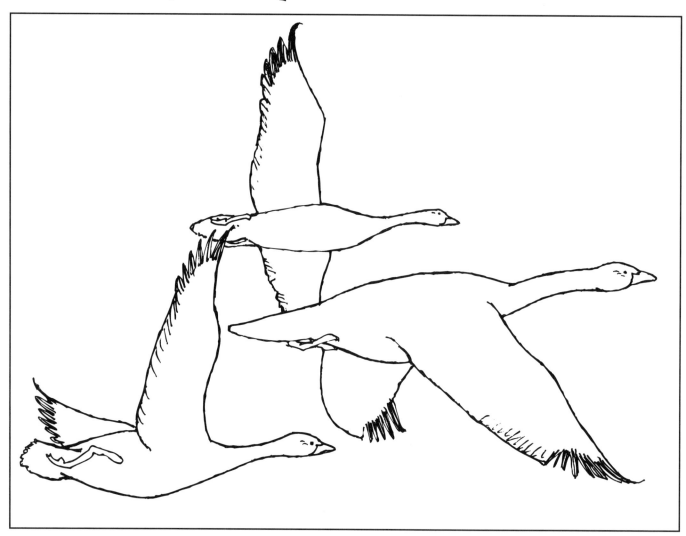

Snow geese fly about 50 miles (80 kilometers) per hour when they migrate.

The journey of some snow geese is 3000 miles (4800 kilometers).

Color the snow geese white with black wing tips.

Color the sky blue.

Snow Geese Migration Route

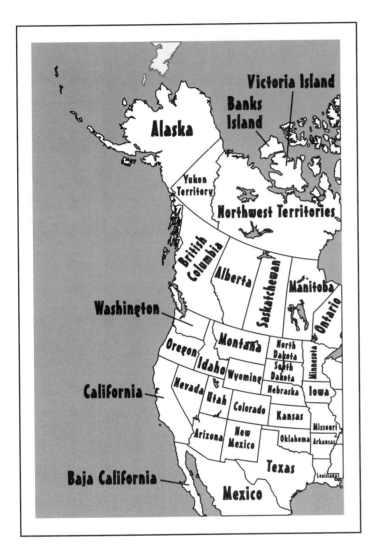

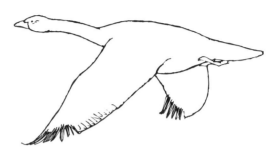

Our snow geese spent the summer on Banks Island, far in the north of Canada. Color this island green.

When the first snow fell, they began the long flight south.

Draw a line on the map to show where these snow geese traveled.

- From Banks Island, the geese flew through the Northwest Territories and Saskatchewan.
- Then they passed through North and South Dakota.
- The next state they flew over was Nebraska.
- After flying through Colorado, the snow geese arrived at their winter home in New Mexico. Color this state yellow.

Note: The activities in this pocket encourage children to think about ways that people get ready for winter.

How We Stay Warm Shape Book

Materials

- pot-bellied stove pattern on page 83, reproduced for each student
- writing form on page 84, reproduced for each student
- scissors
- stapler
- pencils
- crayons

Steps to Follow

1. Discuss ideas for staying warm in the winter. List important words to build a word bank.

2. Have students write about staying warm.

3. Color and cut out the stove; cut out the writing form.

4. Staple the pages together at the top.

Winter Clothing Graph

Materials

- graph form on page 85, reproduced for each student
- 9" x 12" (23 x 30.5 cm) piece of colored construction paper
- crayons
- scissors
- glue

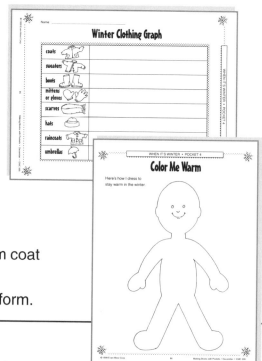

Steps to Follow

1. Sort the winter clothing items found on the classroom coat rack or in the closet.

2. Count each item and make tally marks on the graph form.

Color Me Warm

Reproduce page 86 for each student. Have students color or cut and paste using construction paper to show how they dress in winter.

Pattern of Pot-bellied Stove

How We Stay Warm

Name: _____

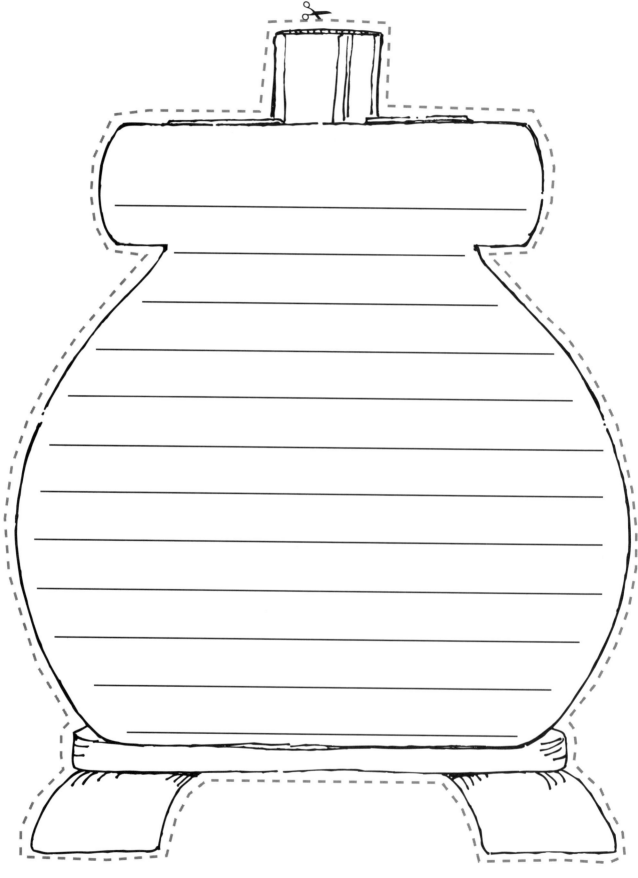

Name: _____

Winter Clothing Graph

	coats	sweaters	boots	mittens or gloves	scarves	hats	raincoats	umbrellas

Making Books with Pockets • December • EMC 595

Color Me Warm

Here's how I dress to
stay warm in the winter.

Note: Reproduce this page and page 88 to label each of the four pockets in the When It's Winter book.

Pocket 1

Some animals hibernate when it's winter.

Pocket 2

Some animals change color when it's winter.

Pocket 3

Some animals migrate when winter is coming.

Pocket 4

People get ready for winter, too.

gloves
heat
snow
mittens
hat
scarf
jacket
stove
boots

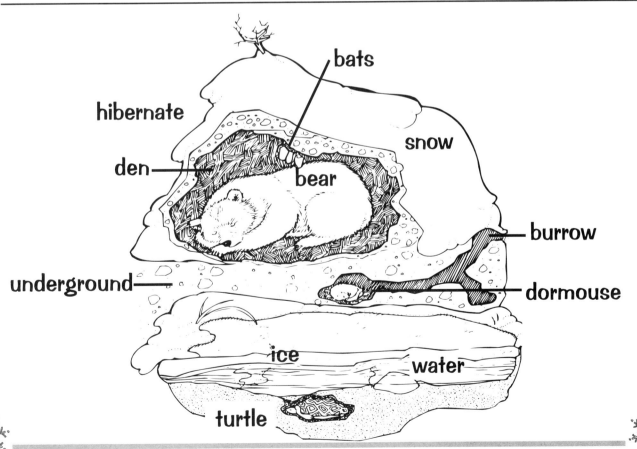

bats
hibernate
snow
den
bear
burrow
underground
dormouse
ice
water
turtle

Name: _____

Bulletin Board
Bonanza

December Is...—pages 92–94

Create a giant December calendar for students to display their ideas about what December means to them.

Materials

- butcher paper to cover a large bulletin board
- cut-out letters—"December Is…"
- writing form on page 93, reproduced for each student
- 7" (18 cm) squares of colored construction paper
- days of the week on page 94, mounted on 3" x 7" (7.5 x 18 cm) construction paper
- scissors
- stapler

Sort It—pages 95 and 96

This interactive board uses snowpeople and snowflakes to give students practice in sorting items using various attributes.

Students sort the objects or pictures provided into two groups and then tell the attribute by which the sorting was done. For example, the snowflake patterns provided might be sorted in the following ways: open/closed, big/little, circles/triangles.

December Is...

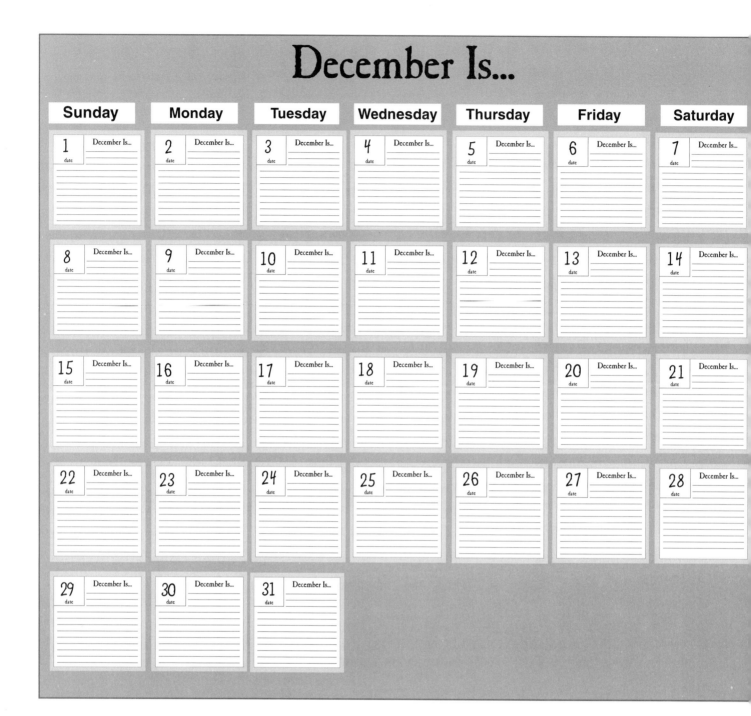

Sunday	Monday	Tuesday	Wednesday	Thursday	Friday	Saturday
1	2	3	4	5	6	7
8	9	10	11	12	13	14
15	16	17	18	19	20	21
22	23	24	25	26	27	28
29	30	31				

Steps to Follow

1. Brainstorm to create a December word bank that students may refer to as they write.

2. Assign each student a date. Students write their dates on the writing form and write about what December means to them.

3. Mount students' writing on colored construction paper.

4. Create the calendar by assembling mounted writing papers in date order.

December Is...

date

Name

Sunday

Monday

Tuesday

Wednesday

Thursday

Friday

Saturday

Making Books with Pockets • December • EMC 595

Give your students practice in sorting by attribute with this festive bulletin board.

Materials

- butcher paper backing—blue
  snow people—white
- bright print wrapping paper for tie and scarf
- 2 real hats
- construction paper scraps for facial features
- envelope to hold sorting cards
- stapler
- push pins
- snowflake patterns on page 96, mounted on 3" (7.5 cm) squares of blue construction paper
- other pictures or real objects to sort

Steps to Follow

1. Create two snowpeople as shown. The size will depend on the size of your bulletin board. Hint: An easy way to draw large circles is to attach a pencil to a piece of string; have a student hold the string on the paper as you circle the pencil to draw a circle.

2. Provide sorting opportunities dependent upon the abilities of your students. The snowflake patterns provided are a fairly difficult sorting task. If you have beginning sorters, put out real objects (various hats and mittens, for example) to be sorted. Move on to pictures as their competence increases.

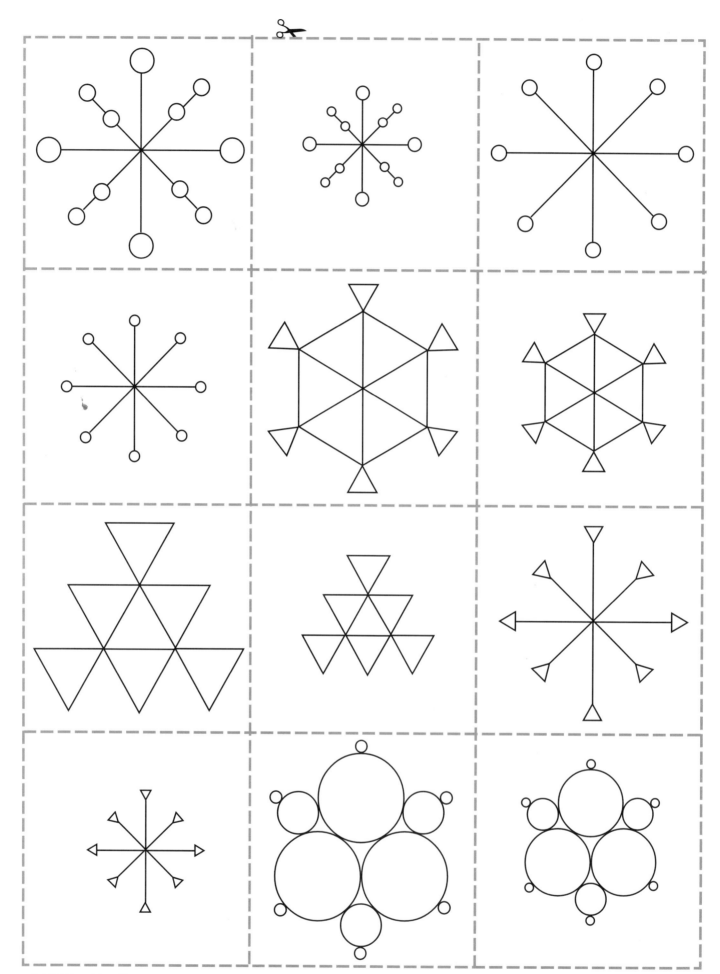

Making Books with Pockets • December • EMC 595